CHEAT SHEETS FOR LIFE

**Over 750 hacks for
health, happiness and success**

AYESHA S. RATNAYAKE

CHEAT SHEETS FOR LIFE

Copyright © 2021 by Ayesha Ratnayake

A portion of this book includes research findings on diet and exercise. It is supplied for informational purposes only and is not meant to take the place of a doctor's advice. Before embarking on any regimen of diet and exercise you should first consult your own physician.

www.cheatsheets.life

For my father, who influenced me to value science.
For my mother, who inspired me to practice kindness.

CONTENTS

WHY I WROTE THIS BOOK

When I was a child, my father encouraged me to read non-fiction. So, in addition to my towers of fiction, I started reading books on science, philosophy, and self-help. And I discovered, between their pages, useful insights that could help me make my life better. As I grew older, I came to love non-fiction even more than fiction, and I started reading deeply about happiness, productivity, and success. I turned my lengthy morning and evening commutes into library visits, listening to audiobooks on my pet subjects, eventually completing over 70 books in a year.

I started jotting down notes from my readings, categorising them according to the area of my life they would benefit. I discovered that, across nearly every dimension of my life, I didn't need to reinvent the wheel. Someone, somewhere, had performed scientific studies to identify which actions produced the best outcomes the majority of the time. In effect, it was possible to derive a handbook for life, based on the efforts of hundreds of researchers.

So that's exactly what I did. After decades spent combing through, saving, bookmarking, and taking notes from research, articles, Yale courses, and hundreds of books, I built the book I've been seeking all my life – a concise handbook of science-backed advice on 17 dimensions of life – from health to money to parenting.

My hope is that, rather than making it up as you go along, you too can benefit from the knowledge I've derived from decades of research. Armed with these insights, I hope you will craft for yourself a life that brings you incredible health, happiness, and success.

HOW TO USE THIS BOOK

In a moment, you're going to be exposed to a wealth of information on the tactics that research shows can point you towards health, happiness and success. You may feel excited to start implementing all these ideas at once. For the perfectionists out there (you know who you are!), I want to assure you that you don't need to act on every single item in order to see big improvements in your life. Even I, as the author, don't practice every one of these strategies!

Instead, I would encourage you to pick out a few ideas that most resonate with you from every chapter, and strive to build these into your life. In some cases, just knowing the best practices will be enough to help you make great decisions that benefit your life. In other cases, you may need to change your habits.

Where a change in habits is needed, remember to start small. Instead of taking on several new habits at once, list them out in order of priority, and then practice the first one until it is a regular part of your routine, before starting on the next. See the chapter on *Motivation* for great pointers on the science of habit formation. You can also download the Cheat Sheets for Life Habit Planner resource by typing cheatsheets.life/#resources into your web browser.

Make this book work for you. Read it in order or skip around to the chapters you think would most benefit you. Treat it as a guide you can pick up anytime you want to perform better in any dimension of life. Finally, I encourage you to explore the *Bibliography* by scanning the QR code or visiting the link at the end of the book to read further on any suggestion that is of special interest to you.

1

Everyday happiness

"Of this be sure: You do not find the happy life...
You make it."
Thomas S. Monson

We all want to be happier. Luckily, while 50% of our happiness does derive from our genetic setpoint, and 10% from our life circumstances, a whopping 40% is determined by our own actions, thoughts, and intentions – it's in our control. Try these practices to build more joy into your life.

COOKING UP INSTANT HAPPINESS

1. **Smile** – Smiling tricks your brain into thinking you must be happy, as much as 2,000 bars of chocolate or receiving 20,000 dollars in cash! Even a fake smile counts. For an even bigger boost, try laughing.

2. **Walk happy** – The way you walk affects your mood. Avoid slouching and walking slowly. Instead, take longer strides, hold your head high, and swing your arms.

3. **Make music work** – Songs with 60-80 beats per minute (but no lyrics) can reduce stress. Find a playlist on YouTube. Actively try to feel happier when listening to upbeat music – it works.

4. **Get out in nature** – Reap the benefits of going green. Just 20 minutes in nature lowers stress hormones. Even a house plant or looking at photos of natural scenes helps you recover from stress.

5. **Savour this moment** – Appreciation is a more powerful predictor of life satisfaction than personality, gratitude, gender, age, or ethnicity. For best results, use all your senses when you savour the moment.

6. **Consider the worst** – Right now, consider all the minor choices and occurrences that had to happen to make the most fulfilling parts of your life possible. Then, imagine your life if they had never happened.

7. **Take photos** – Did you know that taking photos can actually help you enjoy an experience more? Go on – get clicking!

8. **Focus** – You're less happy when your mind wanders than when you're focused on what you're doing. Avoid multitasking and get absorbed.

9. **Rediscover the past** – Reminiscing (even about normal, everyday experiences) can generate a surprising amount of happiness.

10. **Plan a trip** – Planning a trip can make you feel great, even if you don't take it. Design for yourself the perfect day with everything you most enjoy – then go live it!

ADOPTING HAPPINESS HABITS

1. **Practice gratitude** – In a study of character strengths, gratitude was found to be the single best predictor of wellbeing. Start keeping a gratitude journal today to build the gratitude habit.
2. **Bask in the sunlight** – Exposure to sunlight accounts for over 90% of most individuals' vitamin D requirements. Why does that matter? Because Vitamin D naturally boosts mood and helps prevent depression.
3. **Exercise** – Just 20 minutes of exercise can boost your happiness for 12 hours. Meanwhile, exercising in nature can improve mental health in just 5 minutes. And group exercise for 45 mins 3-5 times a week helps mental health most. Also, exercise with motivating music – it will improve your mood by 15%. Hip hop dancers see the biggest happiness boost compared with other exercisers.
4. **Take up yoga or tai chi** – Yoga boosts mood, reduces stress, and improves brain function, while tai chi has similar benefits in reducing stress.
5. **Master mindfulness** – Mindfulness meditation can reduce levels of everyday stress, with longer-lasting effects than a vacation.

6. **Avoid social media** – For most people, using social media reduces happiness and lowers self-esteem. In fact, cutting out social media can have a greater impact on your wellbeing than increased income.

7. **Hit on a hobby** – Hobbies make people happier than escapist leisure like shopping or TV. For the biggest impact, choose a hobby that fully engages you, involves learning a new skill, spending time with others, or doing something nice for someone else.

8. **Read** – Reading reduces stress levels by 68%, which is more than the effect of listening to music, drinking tea/coffee, or walking. And the positive effects emerge within just 6 minutes!

9. **Express yourself** – Making or tending things (especially using your hands) enhances mental health. Baking can boost confidence, and gardening can reduce stress even more than reading.

10. **Find flow** – Strive to take part in activities that are challenging (roughly 4% beyond your current ability is ideal) and yet achievable, where you can see the results of your efforts immediately – this combination increases the likelihood of putting you in a state of optimal experience or "flow".

11. **Be kind** – Do 5 acts of kindness to boost happiness (the effects will be greater if you do them all in one day rather than spread them over a week). Kind acts make people happier than bodily pleasures, especially when done spontaneously and if they involve using one's character strengths.

12. **Volunteer** – 78% of those who volunteer say it lowers their stress levels.
13. **Enjoy a massage** – Getting a massage can reduce levels of the stress hormone cortisol and increase happy brain chemicals serotonin and dopamine by one third.

DESIGNING LIFELONG HAPPINESS

1. **Find a purpose** – Having a purpose for life has been shown to generate the longest lasting form of happiness.
2. **Try fixed role therapy** – 24 hours a day for two weeks, try behaving as though you have the personality traits you would most like to have. They may become part of you.
3. **Use your character strengths** – Those who use their character strengths (the positive ways in which they think, feel, and behave that come easily to them) experience better physical and emotional wellbeing. Take the VIA Character Strengths quiz online for free to find out yours today. Then strive to use them every single day.
4. **Set a daily intention** – One of the most established and validated models of psychological wellness stresses 'autonomy' as the biggest driver of happiness. To introduce more autonomy to your life, decide your intention each day – what do you want to accomplish today?
5. **Act flexible** – Flexible people lead happier lives. Simply acting flexibly can increase your flexibility. 'Luckier' people are open to new possibilities and try new

experiences, listen to their intuition, are optimistic, and look for the good in 'bad' situations.

6. **Curate positive endings** – The ending of an experience matters when it comes to making happy memories, so go out of your way to make the last part of anything the best part.

7. **Restrict pleasures** – Giving up something you enjoy for a while (maybe chocolate?) prevents habituation and intensifies pleasure.

8. **Indulge occasionally** – Guilt over giving into pleasures fades faster than regrets over missing out on the fun. Remember to occasionally choose a little vice over virtue!

9. **Age happier** – Many scientists agree that in general, people get happier with age. 33, 55, the 70s: these have all been called "the happiest age" in various surveys.

10. **Live near what you like to do** – The closer you live to the amenities you enjoy (think within 15 minutes), the happier you are.

11. **Seek blue spaces** – Living within view of water bodies like lakes and the ocean has an even stronger positive effect on mental health than living in sight of greenery.

12. **Improve your circumstances** – Annually track your growth in satisfaction across key areas in your life (e.g. love, profession, play, friends, health, finances, overall) and plan how to make adjustments where needed.

2
Social relationships

*"Life is to be fortified by many friendships. To love and be
loved is the greatest happiness of existence."*
Walter Winchell

As humans, we are social animals that need to feel that we belong – that we are seen, understood, and appreciated. In fact, social relationships have perhaps the greatest bearing on happiness and lifespan. With this in mind, it's a great idea to go out of your way to connect with new people and enjoy the relationships that add value to your life. Whom can you reach out to today?

SEEKING OUT SOCIAL CONNECTIONS

1. **Get social** – Social connection is an important ingredient for wellbeing. In fact, 6-7 hours of socialising per day

leads to the highest levels of happiness. Sharing good feelings and happy memories generates positive emotions.

2. **Build a friend group** – Regular contact with 10 or more friends significantly boosts happiness. Meanwhile, not staying in touch with friends is one of the top five regrets of the dying. So join a group, keep in touch with pals, and accept social invitations.

3. **Treasure happy friends** – Having a happy friend improves one's likelihood of being happy by 15%! Negative attitudes are contagious. Aim to maximise positive connections and minimise interactions with people who drain or frustrate you. Keep your friends close, and your happiest friends even closer!

4. **Find work buddies** – Those who have 3 or more good friends at work are 96% more likely to be very satisfied with their lives.

5. **Seek out happy neighbours** – Happiness spreads rapidly through networks, to the point where when a friend living less than a mile from you becomes happy, your chance of getting happier increases by 25%.

6. **Talk with strangers** – 'Luckier' people have a wide network of acquaintances. Those acquaintances are the ones who send myriad opportunities their way.

OPTIMISING SOCIAL ENCOUNTERS

1. **Forget your phone** – Even having your phone on the table when you're out with friends reduces the pleasure you get from the experience. Put it away y'all!

2. **Act outgoing** – Acting friendly and outgoing makes *both* introverts and extroverts feel better.

3. **Learn to be a listener** – To be a better listener, create a safe and encouraging environment with your manner, make encouraging noises, ask meaningful questions, and be positive and empathetic.

4. **Share memories** – Sharing memories generates positive emotions like joy, accomplishment, amusement, and pride.

5. **Avoid gossip** – Watch your words, as when you gossip about someone else, listeners unconsciously attribute the characteristics you describe about the other person to you.

6. **Embrace hugging** – Hugging helps reduce stress and releases the "love hormone" oxytocin which encourages trust and bonding. Even looking at photos of people being cared for can reduce anxiety.

7. **Surprise them** – Positive surprises make people happier than things they knew about already. Surprise friends and colleagues with unexpected expressions of care.

8. **Dance in a group** – Dancing along with other people boosts mood. The positive effects of regular dance classes can last for up to 8 months after the classes end!

Hip hop dancers top the class in happiness compared with other exercisers.

9. **Sing in sync** – When people sing with others, their heart rates sync up and their breathing steadies, producing a feeling of calm. Go on and join a choir or take your friends to karaoke.

10. **Try rowing** – Rowing with a crew generates a 'rower's high' as you are operating in sync with other people.

11. **Volunteer** – Volunteering makes people feel less lonely. Just 2 hours of volunteering weekly reduced the loneliness level of the recently widowed to that of those who were still married.

12. **Be a reader** – Readers have greater empathy, social perception, and emotional intelligence, and report better social connections and more life satisfaction.

13. **Gift experiences** – Gifting your friends and family experiences will make them happier than gifting them things. Think tickets, vacations, lessons, and memberships. Things that promote positive experiences are good too – think books, sporting goods, and musical instruments).

14. **Learn to say no** – A sense of autonomy is vital to wellbeing, so learn the art of saying 'no'. Start with appreciation, explain in a positive way why you must decline, if possible, offer an alternate contribution which you find manageable, and end with warm wishes.

15. **Get at the truth** – People are more likely to lie when physically tired, so choose early morning for key discussions when their energy is less depleted.

16. **Come to like them** – Want to get over your dislike of someone? Try giving them a thumbs up each day – it will trick your mind into making positive associations with them.

17. **Practice forgiveness** – The act of forgiving has huge health benefits, including less stress and reduced blood pressure. It may help to reflect on the fact that no one is perfect and try to empathise with the other person's individual situation. Journal or tell a friend about your forgiveness.

CONDUCTING EFFECTIVE CONFRONTATIONS

1. **Decide if a confrontation would help** – Experts advise initiating a confrontation if any of the following apply: a promise has clearly been broken; you're frustrated and your body language is sending hostile signals; or when your conscience is nagging you to speak up.

2. **Assume the best** – Due to a phenomenon called fundamental attribution error, people naturally blame their circumstances for their own negative behaviour, whereas they blame character flaws for another's negative behaviour. Instead, ask yourself why a respectable and sensible person might act as the other person did.

3. **Say what you don't mean and what you do** – Anticipate how others might assume the worst and clarify what you don't mean and what you do, e.g. "I don't want you to think I'm unhappy with how we work together. Overall, I'm very satisfied. I just want to talk about how we make decisions."

4. **Describe the gap** – State in plain facts the gap between the expectation and your observation, e.g. "You cut him off midsentence" or "You came in 20 minutes after you said you would".

5. **Tentatively share your story** – Express your story of how the incident made you feel. Remember, this conclusion you arrive at is not fact so share it tentatively and ask for clarification. Say "I'm not sure if I'm correct in my thinking so I thought I'd better check with you.", "Do I have this right or am I missing something?"

6. **Dissipate upset feelings** – If the other person becomes defensive or upset, ask what's bothering them and paraphrase their complaint in your own words to show them you're listening. Restate what you don't mean and what you do and that you're trying to achieve a mutually beneficial outcome.

7. **Apologise** – If you sincerely regret hurting someone, reach out and apologise as it will reduce stress levels in both of you. Avoid the words 'if' or 'but' and don't expect forgiveness. Instead, express regret, accept responsibility and show that you are willing to remedy the situation.

3
Emotional resilience

"If things go wrong, don't go with them."
Roger Babson

Life can be tough and feeling depressed or anxious is a natural response to difficult circumstances. We might feel like we don't want to get out of bed and face the world and even feel unworthy of being a part of society. Here are some practices that can help to alleviate emotional suffering.

RE-EXAMINING DIFFICULTY

1. **Remember you are resilient** – Humans are resilient by nature, adapting surprisingly well to even the toughest life circumstances, even those they predict will leave them devastated.

2. **Turn worry to action** – 85% of the stuff people worry about never actually happen. Even when it does, 80% say they handled it better than they expected. So, turn worrying into planning.

3. **See stress as a stimulus** – Stress boosts focus and can even help improve heart health. People who experience stress but reframe it as excitement ('game on' rather than 'game over') actually perform better than those who don't feel stress at all! Viewing stress as a tool reduces stress-related symptoms such as headaches and fatigue.

4. **Find the meaning** – Those who feel stressed also report having the most meaningful lives. Love, work, parenting, and pursuing goals all involve stress.

5. **Swap setbacks for success** – People who've experienced 5-7 major setbacks have a higher quality of life and greater confidence to weather adversity. In fact, experiencing adversity improves your capacity to appreciate small pleasures and handle physical pain.

6. **Experience post-traumatic growth** – Incredibly, male Holocaust survivors lived longer than men of the same age who escaped Nazi rule. Despite all odds, these survivors experienced post-traumatic growth which enhanced their later years of life.

PREPARING PROACTIVELY

1. **Prepare** – Prepare in advance for stressful situations. Decide now what you would do if specific situations arise in the future, e.g. If X happens, I'll do Y.

2. **Focus on your strengths** – Using your signature strengths can decrease depression for 6 months. Write down 3 things you like about yourself and when a situation arises, ask yourself which of your character strengths you're going to call forward.

3. **Use support apps** – Download apps with science-backed success in providing support, like UpLift for depression or MindEase for anxiety.

4. **Keep a rumination record** – Rumination is a toxic practice of dwelling on negative thoughts. Keep an hourly rumination record to catch yourself ruminating and identify when you ruminate more/less. Prepare to actively distract or relax yourself during trigger periods.

ADDRESSING NEGATIVE FEELINGS

1. **Act calm** – Contrary to popular belief, yelling and behaving violently actually fuels bad feelings. Act calm to feel calm. Paralysis (or Botox!) actually makes people feel less emotional as they can't act out emotions.

2. **Follow your role model** – Acting like someone you admire who has a positive attitude can help you overcome difficult life experiences.

3. **Check your assumptions** – Ask yourself if you're assuming a problem is personal, pervasive, or permanent.

4. **Focus on your values** – Write about how tough experiences relate to your values (e.g. humour, creativity, accepting help). It is a powerful mindset intervention that can boost happiness. Values-focused bracelets and key chains can help even more.

5. **Breathe** – Deep breathing convinces your mind that you're feeling calm. Sit up straight, with even shoulders, and breathe in deeply for a count of five, then exhale completely for a count of seven. Even sighing helps!

6. **Get grounded** – Feeling anxious? Try a grounding exercise: Look around for 5 things you can see, 4 things you can touch, 3 things you can hear, 2 things you can smell, and 1 thing you can taste. This exercise helps you to focus on the present moment.

7. **Change the setting** – A change of scenery can break a spiral of negativity, so simply get up and leave the room, it could do you good.

8. **Find other people** – Time with loved ones puts the breaks on stress caused by rumination (a toxic practice of dwelling on negative thoughts). So, find your people and spend time with them.

9. **Distract** – Distract yourself from negative thoughts. Talk to a friend, watch a funny video, play a video game. Keep a list of engrossing alternate activities to do when you catch yourself ruminating.

10. **Dispute** – Learning to argue with your own negative thoughts will have a big boost to your sense of wellbeing. Start debating with your inner critic.

11. **Distance** – Distance yourself from negative thoughts. Instead of thinking 'I'm sad/mad/etc.', think 'I'm *having the thought* that I'm sad' or try saying the negative thought aloud in a silly voice.

12. **Try Tetris** – Playing the 1980's video game Tetris soon after a bad experience can wipe away bad memories and protect mood!

13. **Try a new perspective** – Consider what you would think about this problem in five years. Consider what a starving child would think about this problem. What would your best self think?

14. **Reinterpret** – Feeling anxious? Pick an upcoming positive experience and tell yourself you are excited instead. Your brain will re-read your anxious symptoms as positive and quell the cycle of anxiety.

15. **Write** – Writing about an unpleasant experience when you're ready to process it can help you move on faster. Writing a negative thought on paper – and then tossing it in the trash – can boost mood.

16. **Heed your hands** – Writing your negative traits with your non-dominant hand and positive traits with your dominant hand boosts confidence.

17. **Write a letter** – Write about how a sad or shameful aspect of your life makes you feel. Then write a compassionate letter to yourself from a kind friend,

including a few lines on changes you can make to improve your life. People typically give others better advice than they give themselves.

18. **Set a timer** – Set a timer to give yourself 5-10 minutes to think through a problem. Then when your timer pings, switch gears.

19. **Take a nap** – Napping may improve frustration tolerance. Try it – you could wake up feeling lighter.

20. **Pride pose** – Stand with your feet hip-width apart and hold your arms over your head. Hold this power pose for over two minutes – it will reduce cortisol and thereby stress.

21. **Help others** – Helping people who are time-constrained helps you feel better equipped to deal with your own time constraints, more so than trying to help yourself. When under stress, to feel better, help more not less.

22. **Chew gum** – The act of chewing gum can help reduce stress levels. For healthy teeth, consider sugar-free chewing gum.

23. **Simply swear** – Surprisingly, swearing can provide relief, especially for physical pain. So, feel free to murmur curses under your breath.

24. **Rewatch a favourite movie** – One study found that people who just thought about watching their favourite movie actually raised their endorphin levels by 27%.

25. **Look for love** – Look at photographs of people being loved or cared for; it can help reduce anxiety.

26. **Heat it up** – People recall fewer negative feelings about a past lonely experience when holding a hot pack. So have some hot tea, take a hot shower, or cuddle a hot water bottle.

27. **Listen to nature** – Listening to the sounds of nature such as ocean waves or chirping birds can help you recover from stress. Look up apps and websites that play nature sounds, and listen in.

28. **Phase out phobias** – To eliminate phobias, start by rating how anxious you feel about the experience on a scale of 1-100. Then practice a relaxation technique like deep breathing while imagining experiencing (or actually experiencing) this event. Continue training yourself to relax till your anxiety rating is less than 10.

EMBRACING SELF-CARE

1. **Seek therapy** – 68% of people say visiting a mental health professional was extremely or very effective in reducing stress. Therapy is most effective in the morning as you are more focused and absorb advice more deeply.

2. **Maintain an active routine** – Not getting out of bed worsens depression. Meet friends, set and go after goals, look after your hygiene, and strive to maintain an active routine.

3. **Have Omega-3s** – Omega 3 fatty acids found in fish and fish oil can help alleviate certain cases of depression.

4. **Meditate** – Meditation is proven to aid depression, anxiety, and chronic pain.

5. **Exercise** – It's a proven remedy for both depression and anxiety. 30-minutes of brisk walking three times a week can be just as effective as medication in alleviating depression.

6. **Walk in nature** – A study showed a walk in nature reduced depression in 71% of participants. 15 minutes can even help you resolve a minor problem in your life.

7. **Create art** – Drawing and painting can improve mood and help you feel greater control over your life.

8. **Dance** – When people with depression dance to upbeat music, they actually feel much better.

9. **Join a reading group** – Reading groups can reduce symptoms of depression and make participants feel more confident, talkative, ready to listen, and interactive.

10. **Get a pet** – Interacting with animals helps to decrease cortisol levels, lower blood pressure, reduce loneliness and boost mood.

4
Health

"He who has health, has hope;
and he who has hope, has everything."
Thomas Carlyle

Everyone wants to lead a life free of pain and suffering. And most of us want to live and be fit for as long as possible. Consider incorporating the following practices into your life to boost your lifespan, fitness, and physiological wellbeing. As always, consult your doctor before making major changes.

DESIGNING A HEALTHY LIFESTYLE

1. **Be happy** – Happy people live longer. In fact, a big smile can add 7 years to your life! Go back and read the chapter on happiness.

2. **But also realistic** – Seniors who overestimate their future happiness have a higher risk of death compared to their more realistic peers.

3. **Find a purpose** – Those who find a direction in life and set goals related to it can live up to an impressive 7 years longer. What's your life purpose?

4. **Rest** – The communities with the longest-living residents have built-in routines to reduce stress. Okinawans pause to remember their ancestors, Ikarians take a nap, Sardinians do happy hour.

5. **Prioritise sleep** – Getting less than 6 hours of sleep can double your risk of death. Sleep flushes out age-related toxins in the brain. So be sure to get your 7-9 hours of sleep. Read the chapter on sleep for more details.

6. **Stop smoking** – It's a leading cause of preventable death.

7. **Avoid the TV** – Every hour of TV-viewing after the age of 25 cuts lifespan by about 22 minutes. Meanwhile, those who watch TV for 4+ hours a day are 80% more likely to die due to heart and arterial disease.

8. **Get grateful** – Patients who kept gratitude journals for 8 weeks showed improvements in heart-rate variability, a measurement of cardiac risk.

9. **Pursue higher studies** – Earning a bachelor's degree or higher can add nine years to your life.

10. **Read** – Those who read books have less cognitive decline and are 17% less likely to die than non-readers.

Reading for at least 3.5 hours per week makes you 23% less likely to die.

11. **Laugh** – Laughing improves heart health and has a similar effect to antidepressants. Bring out the comedies!

12. **Sing** – Researchers in Sweden found that singing improves heart health. What are you waiting for?

13. **Learn something new** – Activities like learning a new language or musical instrument can do wonders for your brain. Ask yourself what it is you would like to learn and get started.

14. **Take up gardening** – There are many mental and physical health benefits of gardening. It is a common hobby among those who live to be 100 years.

15. **Have a pet** – Both cat and dog owners live longer than those without, and experience less anxiety. Consider bringing home a furry friend.

16. **Look after your teeth** – People with gum disease are twice as likely to have heart disease. Get brushing.

17. **Get a mammogram** – 70% of women diagnosed with cancer in their 40s who later died, hadn't had a mammogram. Many women with breast cancer show no symptoms, so mammograms are recommended from your 40s onwards.

18. **Manage anger** – In the two hours following an angry outburst, a person's risk for a heart attack shoots up nearly five times, and the risk of stroke increases more than three times. Learn to manage anger.

19. **Make health a habit** – In order to build habits, first identify the pattern of a cue (a location, time, emotional state, person/people, or preceding action), craving (e.g. to smoke or eat) and reward (the negative activity). Break the pattern by deciding how you'll replace a negative reward with a positive one that satisfies a similar need (e.g. an activity with your hands, a healthy snack).

20. **Use loss aversion** – Due to a psychological tendency called loss aversion, humans naturally hate to lose what they already have more than they love to gain something new. This can be a good motivator! Try apps like LazyJar that make you pay out a sum of money if you don't practice your health habits.

21. **Weigh yourself daily** – The practice of weighing yourself daily is proven to improve weight loss.

22. **Rethink conventional wisdom** – Overweight (but not obese) individuals (with a BMI of between 25 and 29) have a 6% lower risk of death than those of normal or below normal weight. Reasons are unclear, but could be due to doctors being more vigilant about the health risks of overweight individuals.

23. **Don't lose weight to find happiness** – Weight loss doesn't increase happiness even though it may boost your health.

24. **Skip cosmetic surgery** – Those who undertake cosmetic surgery are actually less happy after the procedure than they were before.

25. **Avoid sports fanaticism** – Heart-related deaths can rise or fall in a region depending on how the local teams fare. This is just one of the health risks of being a serious sports fan.
26. **Contemplate death** – An awareness of mortality can promote compassion, align priorities, and encourage the adoption of healthy lifestyle changes.

CONNECTING FOR BETTER HEALTH

1. **Stay social** – A healthy social life is one of the strongest predictors of lifespan, and those with stronger social relationships have a 50% lower risk of mortality. Meanwhile, loneliness is as bad for you as smoking 15 cigarettes a day! The least social people experience memory loss twice as fast. So, interact with others frequently.
2. **Find health-conscious friends** – In communities where people live the longest, being a member of a social circle that supports healthy behaviour is a common thread. Behaviour is contagious – smoking, obesity, happiness, and even loneliness can spread.
3. **Practice family values** – Family togetherness can boost your lifespan.
4. **Build habits together** – People are more likely to stick to a healthy new habit if their partner is trying to make the same change.

5. **Enjoy sex** – Having sex 2-3 times a week means a 45% lower risk of heart disease. Women who enjoy sex may live up to 8 years longer. What's more, couples who had sex three times a week or more can look 10 years younger than those who have sex twice a week or less.

6. **Stay married** – Men who got and stayed married are more likely to live longer (beyond age 70). The effect is present among women too, though less pronounced. It also holds true among gay men.

7. **Parent two kids** – Parents live longer than non-parents, but only if they have no more than two children. Having daughters can boost a man's lifespan (by 74 weeks per daughter!), while a woman who has twins naturally (not as a result of IVF) may enjoy a longer lifespan.

8. **Breastfeed baby** – Women who breastfeed lower their own risk of death from cancer, heart disease, and other diseases.

9. **Model healthfulness** – Parents who meet their health goals are more confident in encouraging healthy habits in their kids.

10. **Attend religious services** – Attending weekly religious services can add a few years to your life. Social integration may play a part.

11. **Volunteer** – Those who volunteer and give back actually live longer, provided they do it for selfless reasons.

MOVING YOUR BODY

1. **Stop sitting** – If you sit for less than three hours daily, on average, your life expectancy could increase by two years!

2. **Move naturally** – The world's longest-living people move throughout the day and walk everywhere. Opt to walk instead of drive, do some gardening, and take the stairs instead of the lift.

3. **Walk fast** – Those who naturally tend to walk fast outlive those who don't by a whopping 8-10 years!

4. **Take the stairs** – Even if you are otherwise inactive, taking the stairs can cut your risk of early death by 15%.

5. **Exercise regularly** – At least 150 minutes of exercise per week can add 4 years to your life. Aim for 30 to 60 minutes of exercise a day (at least 7,500 steps) but avoid polluted areas while exercising as they can do more damage than good. Seniors who exercise regularly can have hearts that look 30 years younger! And heavier people who exercise regularly actually live longer than skinny but sedentary folk.

6. **Add vigour** – A 20:80 ratio for high-intensity exercise to low-intensity exercise is considered ideal. Don't forget to stretch!

7. **Pick your exercise** – Choose a form of exercise you enjoy, which might help you meet interesting people and which you feel you would be good at. These factors will make you more likely to stick to it.

8. **Make it fun** – Make exercise fun by taking scenic routes, strolling through a mall, listening to motivating music (adds a 15% mood boost!), or watching a great TV show while on the treadmill – it will boost your enjoyment and commitment.

9. **Exercise outside** – Outdoor exercise makes you feel more revitalised, energetic, and engaged, and less tense, angry, and depressed.

10. **Choose your exercise time** – Exercising in the morning will boost your mood during the day, help you build strength, keep to your routine, and even burn 20% more fat. Exercising in the evening will mean a slightly more enjoyable workout, better performance, and less chance of injury.

11. **Exercise mindfully** – Paying attention to your body and breathing as you exercise will make you more satisfied with your workout.

12. **Swim** – Swimming can cut risk of dying by about 50% compared to running, walking and being sedentary.

13. **Jog moderately** – Regular jogging can add 5-6 years to your life, with between 1 to 2.5 hours per week at a slow or average pace providing the optimum boost to lifespan.

14. **Pedal fast** – Among cyclists, those who pedal fastest can live about five years longer than those who pedal slowest.

15. **Take up golf** – Golfers tend to have a 40% lower death rate than others of the same age, sex, and socioeconomic status.

16. **Or another recreational sport** – Activities like roller skating, bowling, fencing, volleyball, ping pong, and social dancing all provide an array of health benefits.

17. **Dance** – A study found that frequent dancing reduced the risk of developing dementia by a staggering 76%, more so than any other physical or cognitive activity.

18. **Try exercise snacks** – Even 20-second workouts (e.g. dashing up the stairs) three times a day can generate a significant 5% increase in aerobic fitness.

19. **Walk after eating** – A study revealed the health benefits of walking and light resistance training one hour after eating a high-fat meal.

SEEKING HEALTHY SPACES

1. **Avoid polluted areas** – Long-term exposure to air pollution is linked to increased risks of premature death. 1 in 8 deaths worldwide is linked to dirty air.

2. **Live high up** – The communities with the longest-living individuals live almost 6000 feet above sea level.

3. **Get into the sun** – Sunlight does your body a world of good. So move to or vacation in warmer climes or invest in special sun lights which mimic sunlight to produce its positive effects.

4. **Visit a forest** – A few hours in the woods can lower blood pressure and stress, and boost immunity.

MINIMISING PAIN

1. **Act pain-free** – People who behave as though they are not in pain when under physical pain actually experience less pain.
2. **Power pose to reduce pain** – People in powerful poses (think Superman) can tolerate more pain. Even forming your hand into a fist can help.
3. **Get cussing** – Swearing can provide relief from pain.
4. **Have sex** – The hormone oxytocin, released during sex, is a natural painkiller increasing pain tolerance and reducing pain detection.
5. **Comfort others in pain** – Did you know that giving comfort to others who are experiencing the same pain as you can help reduce your own pain?

OPTIMISING A HOSPITAL VISIT

1. **Visit hospitals in the morning** – Doctors and nurses are dramatically more alert in the morning than in the afternoon so make your appointments early to receive the best care.
2. **Find a good doctor** – Choosing a compassionate doctor can actually help you heal faster.
3. **Secure a view** – Hospital patients with a view of nature tend to have better pain tolerance and recovery rates.

AGEING HEALTHFULLY

1. **Embrace ageing** – Those who have a positive outlook about getting older may live 7.5 years longer than those who view it negatively!
2. **Maintain control in life** – Older people who exert more control over life have better health. So, shop for yourself, tend to a garden, care for a pet, ask for privacy when you need it, set goals, maintain hobbies and interests, attend classes, and meet friends and family.
3. **Act young** – Acting and dressing younger and spending time with younger people can actually keep you physiologically and psychologically healthier, improving memory, blood pressure, intelligence, dexterity, eyesight, and more.
4. **Surround yourself with life** – Older people surrounded by life (plants, animals, and children) experience less boredom and loneliness and a greater sense of purpose. They also live longer!
5. **Look after a plant** – Simply looking after a plant adds immensely to the quality of life of an older person.
6. **Avoid a fall** – Having a fall is the biggest risk to an older person's quality of life. Prioritise good lighting, safe footwear, non-skid surfaces and grab bars, etc.
7. **Seek intellectual stimulation** – A survey of 100 centenarians (people who had reached the age of 100) revealed that 89% rated keeping one's mind active as very important for healthy ageing.

5

Food

*"The food you eat can be either the safest and most
powerful form of medicine or the slowest form of poison."*
Ann Wigmore

We all know that what we consume plays a major role in our
health. The following recommendations will help you ensure
that what you put into your body maximises your nourishment,
lifespan, and physiological wellbeing.

ELECTING WHAT TO EAT

1. **Eat well** – To boost your health and psychological
    wellbeing, eat brightly coloured fruits and vegetables
    (those who eat seven servings of them a day rank the
    happiest), whole grains, olive oil, fish, oatmeal, eggs, flax
    seeds, leafy greens, broccoli, leeks and onions, fortified

grains and grain product, breakfast cereals, kefir, kombucha, sauerkraut, and kimchi.

2. **Snack healthy** – Need a quick snack? Nut-eaters have a 39% lower risk of early death, while walnut-eaters are even better off with a 45% lower risk! Choose healthy snacks such as nuts, berries, bananas, dark chocolate, cheese, yoghurt, wholegrain popcorn, and Greek yoghurt.

3. **Eat beans** – Beans and other legumes (like lentils and chickpeas) have been shown to be the most important dietary predictor of lifespan in people of different ethnicities.

4. **Eat mushrooms** – Seniors who ate mushrooms twice weekly had 50% reduced odds of having mild cognitive impairment. So get smart and eat 'shrooms!

5. **Eat (even inorganic) produce** – It's more important to eat fruits and veggies than to worry if they're organic as the health benefits of organic food are not significant compared to the benefits of eating greens.

6. **Eat (some) fish** – Fish is rich in Omega-3s and can extend your life by 2.2 years. Try two servings per week. Wild salmon is especially good for you.

7. **Eat less meat** – Becoming a vegetarian lowers your risk of premature death by an impressive 12%. Especially avoid processed meats like sausage, bacon, and cold-cuts. Indeed, where people live longest, they eat meat fewer than five times a month.

8. **Cut out sugar** – Reducing refined sugar will help brain health and reduce your risk of developing Alzheimer's disease as well as obesity, diabetes, heart disease, and more. Replace refined sugar with healthy honey.

9. **Avoid burned food** – The chemical acrylamide found in burned food may lead to cancer so avoid eating food that has turned black from cooking or toasting.

DECIDING WHAT TO DRINK

10. **Drink water** – Water is important but you don't need 8 glasses per day. The human body is designed to offer cues which encourage adequate hydration, so use your thirst as an indicator of when to drink. Drink a glass first thing in the morning since you've gone 8 hours without.

11. **Drink tea, especially green tea** – Tea has heaps of health benefits. Japanese people who drink 5 cups of green tea daily had the lowest risk of dying from heart disease.

12. **Drink coffee** – Those who drink three cups of coffee daily tend to live longer than non-coffee drinkers. For best effects, do not exceed five cups and wait 60-90 minutes after waking before your first cup. As the half-life of coffee is 5-6 hours, aim to have your last cup about 10 hours before bed so you can sleep soundly.

13. **Drink hot chocolate** – From helping you think better to boosting heart health, hot cocoa boasts a multitude of health benefits.

14. **Drink red wine** – Alcohol can be a great social lubricant so moderate drinkers can actually live longer than less-social non-drinkers. However, alcohol itself can speed up the ageing process – with one exception, red wine. Those who live the longest drink one to two glasses of red wine per day with friends and/or with food.

ADOPTING HEALTHY EATING PRACTICES

15. **Buy local** – Local food in season is often the healthiest option.
16. **Be aware** – Be aware of how the processed foods industry strives to push you to make poor choices and be conscious of foods and situations you are particularly susceptible to. Opt for real food (grains, fruits, and vegetables) instead of things that come in packaging.
17. **Make it easy** – If unhealthy options aren't in the house and healthy options are, eating healthy becomes both plan A and plan B. So don't buy your trigger foods and instead buy healthy foods that are easy to consume without much preparation.
18. **Cook at home** – Seniors who cooked at home 5 times weekly were 45% more likely to live an extra decade.
19. **Serve precisely** – The brain is wired to want to finish what it started, so serve only as much as you want to eat.
20. **Eat less** – Calorie restriction, intermittent fasting, and time-restricted eating can all improve brain health. With your doctor's okay, try halving your calorie intake on two

non-consecutive days of each week or eating only between 8 am to 8 pm or 12 pm to 8 pm.

21. **Eat mindfully** – To boost happiness, lose weight, and improve your eating habits, put away distractions, eat slowly, and savour every bite. Eat till satisfied, not till full.

22. **Eat socially** – Engage in 'social eating'. Eating meals alone is more strongly associated with unhappiness than any single factor besides mental illness.

23. **Stop at 80%** – In Okinawa, one of the places where communities live longest, they abide by 'Hara Hachi Bu', a guideline to stop eating when they feel 80% full.

24. **Use your non-dominant hand** – Eating with your non-dominant hand can lead you to eat less. Try it for yourself!

25. **Chew more** – Chewing food 40 times instead of the typical 15 times can help you eat nearly 12% fewer calories.

26. **Keep a food diary** – Seeing what you've eaten can actually double your weight loss.

27. **Resist temptation** – Physically pushing away something you seek to resist makes it less desirable to you. Try it with your guilty pleasures.

28. **Try water only** – If practiced appropriately, 24-hour water-only fasts have been proven to increase lifespan. Consult your doctor about trying a 24-hour water-only fast once a month.

29. **Find support** – Social support for your healthy eating habits has a powerful impact on your health outcomes. Whom can you lean on?

6

Sleep

"When I wake up, I am reborn."
Mahatma Gandhi

Getting enough quality sleep is vital to your health and happiness. In fact, poor sleeping patterns can shave years off your life. The following practices can help you design an environment and process that optimises both the quantity and quality of sleep you get.

SETTING UP YOUR SLEEP ENVIRONMENT

1. **Keep it dark** – Pitch darkness fosters the best sleep and improved mental health. Invest in blackout curtains, remove any gadgets, tape over any blinking lights, and wear a sleep mask.

2. **Keep it quiet** – Use earplugs to filter out noise that could disturb your sleep, or if there are disturbing noises, consider using a sound screen or white noise machine to mask them.

3. **Keep it comfy** – Make sure the temperature in your room is comfortable when you wake up. Many sleep experts recommend 18 degrees Celsius (65 degrees Fahrenheit).

4. **Get a rocking bed** – Those who sleep in gently rocking beds fall asleep faster and retain memories better than those who sleep in stationary beds.

5. **Limit your bed use** – Only use your bed for sleep and sex. Using it for anything else (e.g. watching TV) can make it harder to fall asleep.

PREPARING FOR SLEEP

6. **Plan for 7-9 hours of sleep** – Ensure you get 7-9 hours. Getting adequate sleep makes you smarter, more successful, more charismatic, slimmer, more attractive, and much more. Meanwhile, getting less than 6 hours of sleep can double your risk of death!

7. **Go to bed early** – Those who go to bed late are more likely to have repetitive and negative thoughts than those who sleep early.

8. **Get grateful** – Recording 3 things you're grateful for before you head to bed will help put you in a positive

frame of mind and help you fall asleep faster, and sleep longer and better.

9. **Write it down** – If mulling over troubles or a to-do list is keeping you awake, keep a notepad by your bed and jot down what's on your mind or make a list of what you'll do the next day.

10. **Avoid caffeine, alcohol, and cigarettes** – Caffeine, alcohol, and cigarettes all disturb your sleep cycle. Stop drinking coffee at least 10 hours before bed.

11. **Skip fluids before bed** – Good hydration aids sleep but avoid drinking a lot of fluids right before bed as it could lead you to wake up in the middle of the night.

12. **Switch off screens** – For at least an hour before bedtime, avoid looking at digital devices as the light from the screens prompt wakefulness.

13. **Cut out screen light** – Light from digital screens makes you feel wakeful. Install the program Flux on your computer so the light from your screen doesn't interfere with your sleep cycle.

14. **Set up a routine** – A calming bedtime routine, e.g. a warm bath, soporific music and a book (fiction is better for bringing sleep) will prime your body to be ready for bed. Condition yourself to associate specific activities with sleep.

15. **Exercise for better sleep** – Exercise helps sleep, though vigorous activity within an hour of bedtime can make you feel too alert to sleep at night. So consider shifting your routine if needed.

16. **Get sexy** – Engage in sexual activity with a partner or alone before bed as it can help you sleep better.

17. **Put socks on** – Wearing socks can help you fall asleep 15 minutes earlier and wake up far less during the night. A warm foot bath can have a similar effect.

18. **Sleep near Fido** – Women who share a bed with their dog enjoy less disturbance, greater feelings of security, and fall asleep and wake up earlier. Humans and cats aren't as good!

FALLING ASLEEP FASTER

19. **Find a comfortable position** – Finding the most comfortable position to sleep in can help you fall asleep faster.

20. **Relax your body** – Consciously tense and then relax the muscles in your body, starting with the muscles of your face and working your way down to your feet.

21. **Try 4-7-8 breathing** – Inhale for 4 seconds through your nose, hold your breath for seven seconds, and exhale through your mouth for 8 seconds. This ancient yogic breathing pattern is reported to have a chemical-like effect on the brain. Try it three times. Think "I breathe in peace and calm, I breathe out stress and tension."

22. **Meditate** – Meditation can help settle the brain's arousal systems so you get a better night's sleep.

23. **Distract a busy mind** – Focusing on something unimportant and not external can be helpful. For

example, visualise random three-digit numbers floating in the clouds, or inspect the colours (or blackness) behind your closed eyelids.

24. **Use visualisations** – Relaxing visualisations (e.g. floating on a lake in a canoe, lying on a hammock by the beach) can put you in a calm mindset and encourage a good night's rest.

25. **Try to stay up** – Actively trying to keep your eyes open is surprisingly tiring and actually helps you fall asleep. But avoid moving about, looking at your phone, reading or watching TV.

26. **Cure insomnia** – Leave the bedroom if you're not asleep within 15 minutes of going to bed, and only return at a time which will allow you to meet a minimum decided sleep duration (e.g. 5 hours). Once that is successful, keep adding 15 minutes to the decided sleep duration until you are sleeping the desired number of hours. Importantly, your waking time should be consistent each day.

EMBRACING HEALTHY SLEEP PRACTICES

27. **Lie on your back** – The healthiest sleeping position is on your back, though only 8% sleep this way. It removes pressure on your head, neck, and spine and wards off acid reflux. But if you're pregnant, have sleep apnea, or snore, a loosely curled fetal position is a better choice.

28. **Check on snoring** – Check with a doctor to ensure loud snoring isn't a symptom of sleep apnea, a potentially serious sleep disorder.

29. **Follow the 90-minute rule** – Your brain goes through 90-minute sleep cycles during which you move through five stages of sleep. Rather than interrupting a sleep cycle and waking up groggy, time your wake up to be at 90-minute intervals after you fall asleep. For example, if you want to wake at 8 am, aim to fall asleep around 11 pm or 12.30 am.

30. **Let teens sleep in and stay up** – Teens naturally turn into night owls from puberty to their early twenties as their cycles of peak energy shift to later hours.

31. **Cap it at 9 hours** – Sleeping more than 9 hours a night isn't beneficial and can actually increase health risks.

32. **Stop the snooze** – Avoid pressing that snooze button as it actually does more harm than good. Instead, have a morning ritual that you enjoy so you roll out of bed smiling.

33. **Skip weekend lie-ins** – Sleeping in on the weekend won't fix your sleep deficit from the week, and could even be harmful. (Unless you are a shift worker and need it badly.) Instead, try to sleep and wake at the same time throughout the week.

34. **Take naps** – A 10 to 20 minute power nap is ideal for a quick boost as it limits you to the lighter stages of sleep ensuring minimal grogginess upon waking. In fact, regular nappers have better heart health. Get napping!

35. **Nap between 2-3 pm** – The afternoon energy trough of 2 pm to 3 pm is the ideal naptime.

36. **Try a 'Napaccino'** – For the ideal energy boost, try a 'Napaccino' i.e. caffeine followed by a 10 to 20 minute nap.

7
Love

"The best thing to hold onto in life is each other."
Audrey Hepburn

While a romantic relationship isn't a must for a happy and fulfilling life, the quality of the relationships we do have does play a major role in our lives. The following research can help you maximise the joy you derive from your romantic involvements.

FINDING LOVE

1. **Believe it's out there** – Expect that love is out there and that you'll eventually find it. If you embrace the dating process, you are more likely to find the right one for you. Casually get to know a lot of people – even three to five

at a time. Try online dating, attend events, accept invitations, and enlist the help of friends.

2. **Do things you enjoy** – In order to meet people, get involved in activities, groups and causes that spark your interest. When there, don't fixate on your phone – look around, smile, and make eye contact.

3. **Be nice** – Did you know that people who perform altruistic acts are 25 to 46% more likely to find a partner within a year?

4. **Perfect your profile** – 5 or 6 is the magic number of photos to display on your online dating profile. Include both head and (at least 3) full body shots. Eye contact, a bright smile, good lighting and high resolution all help. Share fun and unique facts about yourself, your strengths and what you're looking for. Avoid negativity.

5. **Seek similarity** – Note that despite the myth that opposites attract, the truth is that like-minded people ultimately enjoy easier and healthier relationships with less to argue and compromise over.

BOOSTING ATTRACTION

6. **Boost attractiveness** – Anyone can boost their attractiveness by making eye contact, acting upbeat, dressing well, adding colour to their wardrobe, and being a good listener. Being funny and light-hearted, even slightly risqué, and showing high self-esteem boost

attractiveness. Being around attractive people also makes you seem more attractive.

7. **Get close** – Proximity predisposes people to like each other, so strive to meet the object of your interest often. Even better, coincide meeting them with a time when they are already feeling good (e.g. right after a workout) – they will attribute their positive feelings to you.

8. **Display friend signals** – When people see their friends, they unconsciously smile, tilt their heads to a side, and lift their eyebrows for a moment. Showing these 'friend' signals predisposes people to like you.

9. **Find common ground** – People connect with those who have similar interests, so identify what you and the other person have in common. Ask for information without appearing nosy by first volunteering information about yourself.

10. **Share information** – People like those who reveal their innermost thoughts and feelings, especially if disclosures are emotional rather than factual. But avoid doing this immediately after first meeting the person.

11. **Act like a couple** – People imagine they must be in love when they behave as a couple might, so set up situations where you talk intimately with your would-be partner, give them gifts, stare in their eyes or hang out in the dark together.

12. **Get their heart beating** – A racing heart can be interpreted as love, so take your date on a rollercoaster ride, to a comedy, horror movie, or any other heart-pounding experience.

MAKING LOVE LAST

13. **Choose well, live longer** – Particularly for men (who often don't otherwise have as rich social lives as women), the constant companionship of a life partner can help you live longer. But be sure to choose well as more arguments equate to worse health.

14. **Be great friends** – The determining factor in whether couples feel satisfied with sex, romance, and passion is, by 70%, the quality of their friendship. So be with someone you genuinely respect and admire.

15. **Know your attachment style** – Approximately 54% of people are securely attached, 25% avoidantly attached (tending to avoid intimacy) and 20% anxiously attached (more desirous of closeness). Anxious and avoidant people can become more secure as a result of dating secure individuals. In fact, a four-year study showed 25% of people had changed their attachment style during the period.

16. **Follow the 5:1 ratio** – Happy couples typically have a 5:1 ratio of positive to negative interactions while those that divorce have only 0.8 happy moments for every negative moment. So give your partner a kiss, compliment, or massage. Share a sweet memory. Ask "How can I make your day better?"

17. **Talk more** – The happiest couples spend 5 more hours a week being together and talking.

18. **Respond positively** – Respond to your partner's bids for attention and engagement. Listen to their stories, and heed their requests. How partners respond to good news is even more important than how they respond to bad news – show enthusiasm, ask questions, congratulate, and relive the experience with them.

19. **Be influence-able** – Couples who allow their partners to influence their behaviour are far more likely to stay together. Men, in particular, tend to struggle with this. So, the next time your partner makes a suggestion, think twice before squashing it.

20. **Respect individuality** – A happy relationship involves two happy individuals. Give each other room to explore your own identities, interests, and perspectives.

21. **Have each other's backs** – Making your partner feel protected, cared for, and loved when they are in need is crucial to a happy relationship. Divorce rates soar when this ingredient is missing.

CULTIVATING MUTUAL BLISS

22. **Do something new** – Couples who share new experiences report feeling more affectionate and satisfied with their marriages. How bored you feel today predicts relationship satisfaction a full 10 years later.

23. **Do something exciting** – Long term couples who engage in 'exciting' activities together feel more in love than those who engage in 'enjoyable' activities. Make a

list of what each of you considers exciting – now, go do those things!

24. **Notice the good** – People who wrote down thoughtful things their partner did for 2 weeks felt more connected and more satisfied with their relationship.

25. **Express gratitude** – Say thank you more often to your partner. It will create a positive feedback loop that will enrich your relationship and make it easier to voice concerns in the future.

26. **Practice love languages** – Follow Gary Chapman's advice and figure out if your partner's style of expressing love involves affirming words, physical touch, quality time, gift-giving/receiving, or acts of service. Then show your partner love in their preferred style(s).

27. **Recall shared laughter** – Remembering a time you both laughed together will make you more satisfied with your relationship than thinking back to other positive events.

28. **Hold hands** – Holding hands decreases the levels of stress hormones in your body.

29. **Cuddle** – Cosying up with a loved one releases oxytocin, which helps reduce blood pressure.

30. **Kiss** – Kissing makes you happy and reduces levels of the stress hormone cortisol. 'Nuff said.

31. **Get sexy** – The UK's Living Well Index found that, after sleep, the second most important factor for living well is the quality of one's sex life. The happiest couples have sex two or three times a week. Plus, you'll be healthier –

sex burns 3-4 calories per minute! On a side note, sex with condoms is just as satisfying as sex without.

32. **Wear socks in bed** – Cold feet can be distracting. A study found that 80% of couples wearing socks achieved orgasm while only 50% of the non-sock-wearing couples got so lucky.

33. **Exercise together** – Couples who exercise together report feeling more in love. And couples who start an exercise program together are far more likely to stick to it!

34. **Split chores** – Dishwashing duty is especially important and can have a significant impact on the health and lifespan of a relationship.

35. **Gift thoughtfully** – People generally prefer unique and thoughtful gifts from their partners over lavish gifts.

36. **Double date** – Double dates generate the same chemical reaction as an exotic date night and bring you closer to your partner and another couple.

37. **Deep dive** – Google and ask your partner the "36 questions that lead to love", a series of questions that psychologist Arthur Aron designed to build intimacy. Follow them up with 4 minutes of sustained eye contact.

ADDRESSING CONFLICT

38. **Fight well** – Happy couples defuse the tension when they fight by showing humour, expressing affection, and conceding points, while unhappy couples criticise, show contempt, roll their eyes, tune out and resort to name-calling.

39. **Think third party** – Couples who spent 21 minutes writing about their conflicts from the point of view of an impartial third party saw improvements in their relationship.

40. **Know when to split** – Among those who were genuinely undecided, people who broke up (based on the outcome of a coin flip!) ended up happier than those who stayed in the relationship. If you're genuinely unsure whether to break up, you will probably be happier if you do.

41. **Don't rule out divorce** – Women often thrive post-divorce as they usually have wider social networks than men. However, divorced men's longevity typically takes a hit as many men depend on their wives for social connection.

DESIGNING A HAPPY MARRIAGE

42. **Wait to marry** – Waiting at least 1 year for your relationship to mature before getting married will reduce your odds of divorce by an impressive 20%.

43. **Enjoy marital bliss** – Married people are usually happier than unmarried people, and a happy marriage is worth an additional $105,000 a year in terms of life satisfaction.

44. **Expect a 2-year high** – Marriage leads to a big happiness boost for about 2 years. Thereafter, happiness levels tend to return to what they were before the engagement. To enhance long-term happiness, work on keeping the romance alive.

45. **Marry later in life** – Couples who marry later in life are more likely to stay married. In fact, those who marry at 25 are 11% less likely to divorce than those who marry at 24! More education and income contribute to happy marriages, and personality is still evolving in your 20s.

46. **But not too late** – Past the age of 32, the odds of divorce increase by 5% each year for at least the next decade.

47. **Consider marrying someone younger** – Marrying someone younger can extend your lifespan as it increases the likelihood that you will act and feel younger than you are.

48. **Have an inexpensive wedding** – The more couples spend on their wedding and engagement ring, the more likely they are to divorce! Less than $1000 gives you the best odds.

49. **Boost joy in marriage** – A 20-year study revealed that couples in the happiest marriages have been married 5 years or less, do not have children, have college degrees and the husband is employed.

50. **Reconsider kids** – 67% of couples see a big drop in marital satisfaction following their first baby's birth and they're unhappiest when kids are in preschool. Marital satisfaction usually only increases again once the youngest child has grown up.

51. **Grow happier** – While the first few years of marriage are ripe with conflict, as married couples age, humour (friendly teasing, jokes, and silliness) becomes more prevalent, and bickering and criticisms decline.

8

Parenting

"Speak to your children as if they are the wisest, kindest, most beautiful and magical humans on earth, for what they believe is what they will become."
Brooke Hampton

For many parents, their children are both the most meaningful and the most challenging parts of their lives. Here is what research says about parenthood and the practices that contribute to successful parenting.

DECIDING IF AND WHEN TO HAVE KIDS

1. **Make an informed decision** – If you wanted to have kids and have them, your life satisfaction can increase, but no more than people who choose not to have kids.

2. **Be emotionally ready** – Most new parents become unhappier after their first child is born. In America, parents are typically less happy than non-parents, with happiness peaking again only after the kids leave home. However, in certain European countries, parents report higher levels of wellbeing. Daughters seem to generate less of a drop in wellbeing than sons.

3. **Be financially ready** – Having children increases happiness only when financial worries aren't a factor. The happiness boost is more pronounced when kids are below the age of 10, and less so when kids are between 10 and 14 years.

4. **You've got time** – If you want to conceive your children, while your odds of getting pregnant do decrease with time, they are still over 80% up to the age of 39. However, older parents do have a greater risk (usually less than 1%) of abnormalities in their kids. Consult your doctor on your individual situation.

5. **Older parents live longer** – Having kids in your 40s can increase your lifespan as being around young children makes you feel and behave younger. Older parents are also happier.

6. **Expect to lose sleep** – In the first 2 years of a child's life, parents lose 6 months of sleep, and 10% have only 2.5 hours of continuous sleep per night. Parents report more exhaustion after their first baby's birth than later births, especially if they didn't expect the exhaustion.

7. **Expect earnings to change** – Mothers statistically earn 30% less than non-mothers, while fathers earn 20% more than non-fathers.

8. **Opt for open adoptions** – Adopted adolescents who have ongoing contact with their birth parents are usually more satisfied with their adoptions.

BRINGING UP BABY

9. **Help baby sleep well** – Before 4 months, for safety, have baby sleep in the same room (although not in the same bed) as mum and dad. After 4 months, on average, babies sleep almost an hour more when they sleep in their own rooms. Waiting till they turn one will peak separation anxiety.

10. **Spend time with baby** – Time spent reading, singing, playing, and talking with the baby is crucial to his/her development.

11. **Give them control** – Teach babies that they have control and influence by responding to them, e.g. if they bang the table, you bang the table.

12. **Offer non-electronic toys** – Electronic toys limit quantity and quality of language in infants compared with books and traditional toys like blocks and wooden puzzles.

13. **Give older siblings responsibility** – Give older kids a sense of responsibility and trust, allowing them to hold the new baby the moment it comes home, and to help with

the baby's needs. Praise them abundantly for their support.

PRACTICING POSITIVE PARENTING

14. **Provide unconditional love** – Never tell a child "I love you when you do X" or "I'm so happy when you do Y". Children should know your love is unconditional and your happiness independent of their behaviour. Lack of love leads to hostility and emotional instability.

15. **Be nurturing** – Pre-schoolers with nurturing mums have a 10% larger hippocampus (the part of the brain which handles stress and memory). Meanwhile, feeling loved by one's dad is even more important for wellbeing. Love in abundance minimises sibling rivalry.

16. **Protect your own happiness** – A mum's satisfaction with her life matters more to a child's emotional/social skills than her education, income, whether she has a job or how much time the kid spends in day-care.

17. **Recognise personalities** – Older siblings usually imitate parents and are responsible. To be different, younger siblings tend to be rebels or use humour. Middle children are more likely to be diplomatic. But remember that each child is born with a unique personality with different characteristics and temperaments and needs to be understood and nurtured differently.

18. **Adjust parenting styles** – If a child can regulate her own emotions and actions, she'll need less structure and more autonomy. If she's poor at self-regulation, she'll need the

reverse. A mismatched parenting style doubles the chance a child will be anxious or depressed.

19. **Practice love languages** – Follow Gary Chapman's advice and figure out if your child's style of expressing love involves affirming words, physical touch, quality time, gift-giving, or acts of service – then show your child love in their preferred style(s).

20. **Talk intimately** – If you want your child to talk to you about anything, share the details of events from your day, your life and childhood, and describe how you felt.

21. **Respect introversion** – Don't assume your quiet child is being difficult. Understand that introverts' brains are wired differently.

22. **Introduce family rituals** – Kids who have regular family dinners usually turn out happier and more successful. Early on, introduce rituals like shared meals, outings, chores, volunteering, etc.

23. **Avoid rushing first grade** – Starting first grade before the age of six is linked to a shorter lifespan.

24. **Schedule downtime** – Both kids and adults need time to just do nothing so don't overschedule your child. Sharing play and downtime with your child is even better – it's good for both of you.

25. **Restrict digital media** – The happiest teens use digital media (i.e. social media, TV, video calls, texting) for less than 1 hour/day. Meanwhile, teens who spent 5+ hours a day online were twice as likely to be unhappy. And every

additional hour of TV led to an 8% increase in depressive symptoms.

26. **Cultivate hobbies** – Help your child find hobbies and take them along when you explore your own interests (e.g. to museums, to support causes, to exercise, to volunteer). Having hobbies can reduce susceptibility to drugs and depression.

27. **Shape the space** – Keep interesting books, magazines, creative toys, and instruments around for your child to easily engage with, but don't push them too hard to engage.

28. **Encourage physical activity** – Playing sports makes kids happier and better behaved. And tweens who believe they're good at sports have higher wellbeing (more than kids who really are!).

29. **Gift experiences** – Reward your child with experiences, not things, as materialism leads to dissatisfaction and depression. Meanwhile, experiences make people happier than things.

30. **Walk to school** – Walking improves concentration. Students who walk to school are more ready to learn.

31. **Go green** – Growing up near green spaces benefits mental wellbeing, reducing the risk of later developing mental disorders by 55%.

32. **Get outside** – Children who spent more time outside and feel more connected to nature report feeling happier. Seek out parks, forests and playgrounds!

CONVERSING WITH KIDS

33. **Listen, don't lecture** – When your child talks to you, don't ask questions, downplay the problem, philosophise, show pity or advise. Instead, simply listen with full attention, acknowledge feelings, and give their feelings a name. Empathetic silence is often all they need.

34. **Avoid saying 'no'** – Consciously seek alternatives to the word 'no'. Move things out of reach, distract, say 'Gentle', 'We'll add it to your birthday wish-list', etc. Save 'no' for hard noes like dangerous activity.

35. **State, don't scold** – When you want a child to do something, simply provide information, e.g. "The light is on in the bathroom" (instead of "Switch off that light"), "Milk turns sour when not refrigerated" (instead of "Who left the milk on the counter?), "I don't like having my sleeve pulled" (instead of "Stop that").

36. **Emphasise values over rules** – Parents of ordinary children have an average of 6 rules. Parents of highly creative children have an average of 1 rule, instead emphasising values like respect, integrity, perseverance, and creativity. Correct after the fact rather than setting rules at the outset.

37. **Keep it positive** – Always use a positive or neutral tone when asking a child to do something and never ask more than twice. A gentle tone and expression and using the word 'please' gets the best results while a harsh tone or nagging increases deviant behaviour.

38. **Be specific** – When asking a child to do something, be very specific. "Clean your room" is not specific but "Please pick up all your toys and put them in the toy box" is more so.

39. **Go down to eye level** – Getting down on your knees to the child's eye level will make the child more likely to listen.

40. **Offer choices** – Offer kids choices whenever you can (e.g. "Please put on your green sweater or red coat"). It will greatly increase the likelihood that your child will listen.

41. **Offer help** – Offering assistance will increase the likelihood your child will listen (e.g. "Please bring your book to the table, I'll help you figure out your assignment.")

42. **Playfully challenge** – With a cheeky smile say "I'll bet you can't do that in under a minute, you'd have to be a superhero!" to reinforce a positive action.

43. **Create positive peer pressure** – Kids who are told that others like them usually do things a particular way are more inclined to act the same way.

44. **Channel a character** – When small children pretend to be a favourite character, they perform better on challenging tasks, including managing their emotions.

45. **Use tokens** – Rather than punishments, offer your children positive rewards for good behaviours in the form of tokens (stars/points/stickers which can be cashed in for special foods, activities, or privileges). Withhold these

when they do not listen. Explain the token system clearly, review it daily, and never withhold earned rewards (or the system breaks down).

46. **Leverage praise** – Praise can be used to effectively change behaviour. Effusively praise even increments of good behaviour immediately, be specific about the action and give non-verbal affirmation (like a hug, pat, fist bump, or high five).

47. **Praise to build character** – Praise effort over ability or intelligence. Otherwise, kids may struggle to cope with failure. Rephrase good behaviours in character contexts, e.g. "It looks like you're the type of person who likes to help others" rather than "That was nice of you".

CHANGING BEHAVIOUR

48. **Shape behaviour** – If you want a big behaviour change, start by asking for a very small one (you can help with it) and praising that behaviour, then gradually work up in increments, e.g. from studying for 10 minutes per day to eventually studying for an hour a day.

49. **Bypass meltdowns** – When children want something you can't give them, instead of giving them logical explanations as to why they can't have it, fantasise with them about how you wish you could give it to them.

50. **Use a 3-part reprimand** – Tell the child what to stop, why stop, and what to do instead. Stating rationally why

the behaviour is inappropriate gives respect to kids and teens and helps them internalise the lesson.

51. **Try time out** – 'Time out' (where a child is briefly sent to a boring place when a problem behaviour occurs) really works. Limit time out to 5 minutes as extending this period does not make time out more effective.

52. **Withhold treats** – Briefly withholding privileges works. More important than what's withheld is the immediacy after the negative behaviour occurs and follow-through.

53. **Avoid spanking** – Interventions like hitting and spanking can actually increase non-compliance, and can have harmful side effects such as increasing overall aggression.

54. **Consider ignoring** – Similar to starving a fire of oxygen, ignoring a repeated unwelcome behaviour can help eliminate it. Sometimes even an atmosphere of heavy expectation can cause a child to resist.

55. **Don't stress** – Don't worry even if children don't behave perfectly. The occasional slip-up is fine and won't cause a slippery slope. Avoid putting pressure on kids to be perfect.

56. **Simulate good behaviour** – Daily, over a week, invite your child to play a game where you set up a situation (e.g. you saying no TV time) where they usually react with negative behaviour (e.g. hitting) and challenge them to respond differently, specifying the desired actions (e.g. no hitting). When they perform, praise them effusively, and playfully challenge them to try it again.

57. **Try the veggie challenge** – Ask children to rate which vegetables they hate most and then challenge them to try to eat three portions a week over three weeks. They typically then rate the veggies as less awful thereafter since they've seen themselves eating them.

CULTIVATING CHARACTER

1. **Be a role model** – List out characteristics you'd like your child to have (e.g. kindness), list concrete examples of what it looks like, then model those behaviours (or point them out when you see them) and state what was done, then praise kids if you see them do it too.

2. **Demonstrate optimism** – Kids pick up on how their parents react to problems. Those who learn to be optimistic when they're 10-12 years old are half as likely to be depressed during puberty.

3. **Cultivate kindness** – Children who are kinder to others are happier. Kinder pre-teens are also better liked by classmates. Parents who encourage kids to be kind rather than to get good grades have happier kids who actually do earn higher grades!

4. **Encourage empathy** – Children who are accepted as they are by their parents feel more compassion. Ask your child to imagine being someone else. Praise their kindness towards others. As a parent, model empathic behaviour by forgiving others' mistakes.

5. **Build emotional intelligence** – Teach your child to recognise emotions, practice optimism, and adopt relationship building skills.

6. **Illustrate friendship** – Adopt Brené Brown's tactic of telling your kids to think of their peers as each having a marble jar; when a peer is kind, the peer's marble jar fills up, when he/she is mean, he/she loses marbles. Teach them to spend time with those with full marble jars.

7. **Welcome peers** – Welcome your child's peers into your home and on excursions to expand the influence of home on the child's life.

8. **Practice gratitude** – Grateful teens have more self-control and are less likely to abuse drugs and alcohol. Introduce a nightly gratitude practice into your home.

9. **Strengthen savouring** – Cultivate the skill of savouring. Encourage kids to use all their senses and take a 'picture memory' whenever they are really happy.

10. **Stimulate creativity** – When playing, encourage kids to think outside the box and create something unique. If they draw a green sun, celebrate it. Ensure they know there are no dumb questions/ideas.

11. **Cultivate meaning** – Even 8-year-olds are happier if they feel their lives have meaning. Encourage kids to do kind deeds, plan events, volunteer, and join teams.

12. **Introduce chores** – Help your child feel participation is natural by enlisting their help in chores from an early age. Convey that their responsibilities will increase with age, and strive to align chores with the kid's core strengths.

9
Money

"Every time you spend money, you're casting a vote
for the type of world you want to live in."
Anne Lappe

Almost all of us want more money, but accumulating material possessions doesn't actually make us happier. Nonetheless, there are other ways in which to spend money that do boost happiness. Discover them here alongside advice from the world's richest on how to maximise your wealth.

CONSIDERING EARNINGS

1. **Don't work for money** – When it comes to careers, the biggest regret is taking a dissatisfying job just for the pay. Indeed, while income can alleviate emotional pains and therefore improve life satisfaction, it does not elevate day-

to-day happiness levels. In fact, people with more wealth aren't as good at savouring the positive. Even lottery winners aren't significantly happier than other people. So seek financial stability but don't pursue wealth in place of purpose.

2. **Cap your earnings** – A study found that $75,000 a year is the maximum household income that boosts day-to-day happiness, even in expensive cities. This value is lower for less wealthy regions, dropping to $35,000 in Latin America. Incomes beyond satiation point can actually negatively impact life satisfaction, perhaps because they affect relationships.

3. **Boost your pay** – Switching jobs 3-5 years after you've started is one of the best ways to boost your pay.

4. **Leverage creativity** – People whose work is "above average" for creativity have household incomes 15 times greater.

5. **Vacation for a raise** – People who use up their vacation days have better performance and are more likely to get a raise.

AVOIDING UNREWARDING PURCHASES

6. **Stop buying stuff** – Material things do not generate lasting happiness, as due to hedonic adaptation, people stop valuing these items with time. Among material purchases, jewellery generates the lowest gratification.

And watch out – more materialistic people tend to be less happy.

7. **Don't upgrade your car** – There is no relationship between the price of a car and the enjoyment you get from driving it. Also, drivers of expensive cars are more likely to break traffic rules – don't be that guy!

8. **Spend less on your wedding** – The more couples spend on their wedding and engagement ring, the more likely they are to divorce. Less than $1000 gives you the best odds.

PURCHASING HAPPINESS

9. **Spend on experiences** – Experiences will make you happier than things. You will be able to joyfully anticipate the experience, enjoy it in the moment, and reminisce fondly about it. And if you pay in advance, you'll enjoy the moment more. To create even more happiness, make it a social experience – a vacation with family or friends offers the highest gratification.

10. **Buy back time** – Spending money to buy back time could make you happier. For example, hiring a cleaning service or a babysitter, or outsourcing your grocery shopping.

11. **Give** – The more you spend on others (called 'prosocial spending') the happier you are. In fact, giving to others, especially loved ones, makes you happier than splurging on yourself.

12. **Donate** – Across 136 countries, donating to charity had a similar impact on happiness as doubling household income. Wow!

SECURING YOUR SAVINGS

13. **Drop overspending friends** – Avoid spending time with peers who spend lavishly and who encourage you to do the same.

14. **Use cash, not cards** – Using physical cash for purchases makes you more conscious of what you spend than paying by card.

15. **Watch less TV** – Every hour people spend watching TV, they spend $4 more per week and feel less satisfied with their income as they try to keep up with the unrealistic lifestyles shown.

16. **Try an ageing app** – People tend to save more when they see aged pictures of themselves or adopt an older avatar on an online video game. Try it out to develop a more prudent mindset.

17. **Avoid lifestyle inflation** – Stay in the green by spending the same amount even as you make more money. Avoid the trap of unnecessary spending as your income grows.

18. **Secure your wallet** – Including a photo of a cute, smiling baby in your wallet increases the chances of it being returned if lost! And don't forget your address.

19. **Set up a will** – Decide on beneficiaries, who'll raise your children, and who'll deal with your will. Leave things that

would be taxable to charities and those that wouldn't be to your kids. Set up a trust to manage disbursements to beneficiaries and enjoy tax exemptions.

INVESTING IN FINANCIAL FREEDOM

20. **Find financial freedom** – Invest in stocks, bonds, mutual funds, notes/IOUs, income-generating real estate, funds from your intellectual property, and businesses that don't require your active presence. Anything desirable that produces income or appreciates will be a valuable source of passive income.

21. **Choose index funds** – In the USA, index funds (which invest in a basket of companies) outperform mutual funds 80% of the time. Even Warren Buffet has instructed that after his death, his money should be invested in low-cost index funds.

22. **Diversify your portfolio** – Minimise risks by diversifying across asset classes (stocks, bonds, real estate), within asset classes (e.g. individual companies in a class), across countries, and time.

23. **Rebalance your portfolio** – Rebalance your portfolio every 6 months. If you allocate 60% to stocks and 40% to bonds, if the stocks have shot up over 60%, sell the excess to rebalance.

24. **Invest early** – Start investing as soon as possible. Investing a small amount at age 19 can generate more

returns than investing 10 times that amount at age 27 at the same rate!

25. **Get the best help** – Hire a registered financial advisor who is not personally nor via his/her company affiliated with a brokerage or paid to recommend particular investments. Ensure your money is held with a separate independent authority and invested in index funds. Ask your advisors to ensure any trades they bring you offer disproportionate reward versus risk.

26. **Pay attention to tax** – Or you may be in for nasty surprises!

27. **Expect drops in the market** – They usually don't last. Plan to stay the course. The pendulum will swing, so the best opportunities often occur in times of pessimism. Warren Buffet says the stock market is a way of transferring money from the impatient to the patient.

28. **Remain unemotional** – Learn to ride the waves of emotional impact about changes in the market. Pre-define the get-out points where you expect others would panic and try to leave. Decide in advance how you will react.

29. **Embrace a crash** – Market crashes are a great opportunity to make money. If you experience a once-in-a-lifetime chance to buy great stock at low prices, grab it.

10

Learning

*"The illiterate of the 21st century will not be those
who cannot read and write, but those who cannot
learn, unlearn, and relearn."*
Alvin Toffler

Both formal and informal learning occupies a great deal of our
time and can contribute immensely to the quality of our lives.
The following practices will help you to extract the most value
from your learning experiences.

SELECTING WHAT TO LEARN

1. **Choose what to learn** – All knowledge is not created
   equal. Developing skills like planning, goal-setting,
   learning, communication, managing energy, changing

behaviour, and overcoming cognitive biases could serve as lifelong investments.

2. **Learn diverse subjects** – Those with skills across multiple subjects tend to be more successful and creative in life. And studying different subjects together can actually improve learning across all of them.

3. **Filter learning material** – Read reviews to filter the best learning material and be willing to drop material midway if it's not up to par. Read the article abstract or the first three chapters of a book and then evaluate whether it's worth continuing.

LEARNING HOW TO LEARN

4. **Learn every minute** – Always be learning. Use reading apps. Leverage audiobooks and videos to learn as you eat, commute, do chores, etc. Increase playback speed to consume material faster. Research shows that you can learn and retain just the same from listening as reading.

5. **Have a growth mindset** – Believing that your abilities can be developed (that it's okay to still be learning and you will improve with effort) is linked to greater success in all aspects of life.

6. **Get enough sleep** – It significantly aids learning. Deep sleep (in the first half of the night) is good for memorising hard facts while sleep in the morning hours aids creativity.

7. **Get some exercise** – Exercise boosts learning both directly, by growing the parts of the brain that control

thinking and memory, and indirectly, by improving sleep, mood and wellbeing.

8. **Drink water** – Water helps improve overall mental processing.

9. **Start school late** – Later start times benefit teens in many ways, including improving grades, reducing depression, and minimising vehicle accidents. The optimal time for college classes is after 11 am.

10. **Don't stress over grades** – Whether they're higher or lower than expected, your grades barely affect your ongoing happiness. So, learn for pleasure, not for grades.

11. **Read mindfully** – Pause and reflect on how you can apply useful points, look up anything unfamiliar, act on anything immediately actionable, make and revisit notes, remember the key jargon, discuss the material with a friend, and consider reading the source material.

12. **Write it down** – Humans can only hold 3-4 items in their thinking at a given time. Each new item pushes out another, so write things down.

13. **Write, don't type** – Those who type notes process the information at a shallower level than those who write them by hand. Put the laptop aside and go manual.

14. **Use your own words** – Don't transcribe verbatim. Writing notes in your own words boosts test performance.

15. **Space it out** – Cramming limits your chances of remembering what you studied. It's better to do an hour today and an hour day after rather than everything all at once.

16. **Take breaks** – 5 to 10 minute study breaks improve learning, while a 20 to 30 minute break before a test can have the equivalent effect on test scores of an additional 3 weeks of learning.

17. **Test before you learn** – Doing a test on a subject before you know anything about it improves learning.

18. **Take a nap** – Napping is good for learning capacity. There you go, another reason to take a nap!

19. **Embrace distractions** – Distractions aren't all bad when it comes to learning and can even benefit the process.

20. **Reward yourself** – Rewards boost learning due to the release of dopamine. So treat yourself when you meet your learning milestones.

21. **Test yourself** – Testing is much more effective in creating retention than simply studying. It also shows you the gaps you need to revisit, helping you fill them.

22. **Teach it to a friend** – Identify the gaps in your understanding of a topic by explaining it to a friend, writing a blog post about it, or pretending to teach it to a 6th grader.

23. **Sum it up** – Try to express the core learning within 280 characters (or two tweets). This can help you to focus on what is truly essential about the idea.

24. **Read contrarian views** – If there are contrasting views on a topic, seek out experts expressing varying viewpoints and note the points where they agree and where they disagree to inform your judgment.

25. **Study an expert** – Ask questions and learn from an expert, online or in person, who can explain their thinking as they execute their skill.

26. **Practice deliberately** – Instead of mindless repetition, specifically focus on measuring and improving performance with each practice.

MAKING LEARNING MEMORABLE

27. **Do it halfway** – The human brain yearns to close open loops, so almost-done projects tend to linger in memory longer than completed ones. Take advantage of this when you want to hold something in mind.

28. **Mix up the format** – To better remember content, use varied learning locations, and review in various ways at different times of the day. Using different learning strategies significantly boosts the learning of motor skills as well.

29. **Make it a picture** – Recall of pictures improves over time while recall of word lists weakens. So try creatively converting abstract ideas into concrete images.

30. **Use a mnemonic device** – Mnemonic devices help in recalling long strings of information, e.g. the name 'Roy G. Biv' to recall the colours of the rainbow – red, orange, yellow, green, etc.

31. **Chunk it** – Break down what needs to be remembered into groups or chunks – you'll remember it better. For example, 347-295 is easier to remember than 347295.

32. **Make it weird** – The weirder the picture or wording used to recall something, the more memorable it will be. Make it wild, exaggerated and even lewd.

33. **Make it useful** – Relevance matters a lot to memory (the mundane is forgotten, the useful remains). Consider how you can use the information in your life to make it stickier in your mind.

34. **Say it out loud** – Lists read out loud are recalled more frequently than those read silently.

35. **Space out reviews** – Review what you just learned shortly after learning it, then space out the reviews afterward at increasingly longer time intervals. You can then adjust the frequency of reviews based on how much you were able to recall.

36. **Match the environment** – Recall is better in similar environments to the environment where the material was learnt. So, try studying in the exam hall or practicing the speech on stage.

37. **Mix up your study spots** – Studying material in several places will help you remember it better as you'll have multiple contexts to associate it with.

11

Work

"Far and away, the best prize that life offers is the chance to work hard at work worth doing."
Theodore Roosevelt

Given that a major portion of our lives is devoted to the work that we do, having a positive experience while we work is a significant contributor to our overall wellbeing. Follow these suggestions to elevate your experience of work.

BOOSTING ENJOYMENT AT WORK

1. **Use your strengths** – Using 4 or more of your character strengths at work will improve your work life. 81% of people who've had strengths-based career counselling are employed compared to 60% of people who've had conventional career counselling. Take the VIA character

strengths quiz online for free today to discover your strengths.

2. **Discover meaning** – You'll enjoy work more if you find meaning by using talents, striving to help others, and growing into your dream job.

3. **Work hard** – Did you know that people with conscientious, hard-working personality traits can live about two to three years longer?

4. **Pick a creative career** – People in creative careers have the health equivalent of someone 6.7 years younger!

5. **Know what matters** – Men say compensation and interest in the work maximise satisfaction, while women get the most satisfaction from flexibility, workload, advancement, and the people at work.

6. **Bond with work buddies** – If you have 3 or more good friends at work, you're 96% more likely to be very satisfied with your life. Meanwhile, lone wolves have a 2.4 times greater mortality risk.

7. **Spread kindness** – Doing kind things for co-workers makes you and the recipients feel more control at work and sparks more kindness.

8. **Get 'me time'** – Getting time to yourself makes you happier, more engaged, and more productive at work.

9. **Set boundaries** – A sense of autonomy is vital to wellbeing, so set the boundaries of what you are not willing to do, e.g. remain online while at home.

10. **Commute less** – A shorter commute will make you more satisfied with your job. In fact, long commutes are

draining in a way that a bigger house or better job cannot compensate for.

11. **Walk or bike to work** – Car commuters are more likely to report a harder time concentrating and being under constant strain.

12. **Personalise your space** – Personalising your space with objects, photos and awards can boost your happiness and your satisfaction with your job. Plants especially make you happier.

13. **Use a standing desk** – Adjustable standing desks make you happier, healthier and even 46% more productive. So use a standing desk (or elevate your computer with a pile of thick books).

14. **Avoid the nightshift** – Shift work has been linked to obesity, heart attack, a higher rate of early death, and even lower brain power.

15. **Evaluate a job change** – If you have more than two 'no' responses to these questions, you are likely to be better off quitting your job: Do you want to be in this job on your next work anniversary? Is your job both demanding and in your control? Does your boss allow you to do your best work? Does your daily work align with your long-term goals? Either way, if you're seriously considering it, you are more likely to be glad than unhappy if you take action.

16. **Postpone retirement** – People who work at least a year past retirement age have an 11% lower risk of dying. Working into your 70s is even better.

CONDUCTING BETTER MEETINGS

1. **Meet in the morning** – People are more alert and agreeable in the morning and dramatically less so in the afternoon. Set up meetings during the morning hours.

2. **Have 45-min meetings** – Asking for 45-minute rather than 1-hour meetings will keep energy levels high.

3. **Host standing meetings** – Standing during a meeting can improve teamwork, creativity, and problem-solving.

4. **Suggest walking meetings** – A technique of Steve Jobs which has been validated by research, walking meetings can be particularly productive as the exercise benefits your thinking.

MAKING GOOD IMPRESSIONS

5. **Dress right** – Dress the way you want to feel and to be seen. Dressing professionally makes people see you as more credible, and dressing creatively makes you feel more creative.

6. **Sit in the middle** – Sitting towards the middle of the table in a meeting boosts your chances of making a good impression.

7. **Stock up achievements** – To create the best impression as you enter a new group, avoid being very assertive until you've stockpiled a few achievements.

8. **Express leadership** – The first one to talk in a group is the one typically perceived as the leader.

9. **Get the right support** – If you seek support for a radical new idea, the worst person to ask is a middle manager. Instead, look to an entry-level employee or senior executive.

10. **Reframe** – Are you nervous about a big presentation? Tell yourself out loud that you're "excited" instead – you are likely to do even better than if you weren't nervous at all.

11. **Swear occasionally** – Curiously, profanity can actually promote trust and teamwork in the office!

12. **Take vacations** – People who use up their vacation days are more likely to get a raise. Vacationers are happier, less stressed and more successful at work and home.

12
Motivation

"Today is your opportunity to build the tomorrow you want."
Ken Poirot

Each of us has goals we hope to achieve, personally and professionally. Yet often we find ourselves avoiding taking the actions that would help us make progress on our goals. The following practices can help you overcome the urge to procrastinate and encourage you to take action.

SETTING GOALS EFFECTIVELY

1. **Set goals** – Wish you were doing more in life? List your top 25 goals, then circle the top 5 and plan how to achieve those. Ignore the rest till those 5 are done – completing a few meaningful goals creates more fulfilment than many half-finished projects.

2. **Set happy goals** – Be aware that goals focused on making more money, getting a better job, enhancing your physique, or acquiring more stuff will not make you happier. Anchor your goals in your values.

3. **Set stretch goals** – Experts recommend setting goals with about 50-70% chance of success. Stretch goals that demand effort excite fear, energy, and excitement!

4. **Set a deadline** – Tasks with a hard deadline are more likely to be completed than those without one. But note, deadlines on creative tasks can sometimes reduce intrinsic motivation and flatten creativity, so use them carefully.

5. **Make it feel close** – You are more likely to procrastinate on a goal if it bleeds into the following calendar week, month, or year. Set deadlines that feel close and pressing.

6. **Start afresh** – Take advantage of 'new mental accounting periods' like a new year, the first day of the month or week, a holiday, or a birthday. These days create new perspectives and improve motivation.

7. **Leverage turning points** – At the end of a decade, people are usually more motivated to make a change. Disproportionately more marathons are run at ages 29, 39, 49, etc.

8. **Imagine a new you** – As you start something new, think of yourself as a new person. It will boost your motivation.

9. **Avoid false motivators** – The science is in! Celebrity role models, willpower, desire suppression, and

visualisations (positive or negative) don't work to motivate you.

10. **Instead, set smart goals** – Concrete, measurable, realistic, and time-based goals with step-by-step plans to achieve them (with up to 5 smaller steps) are what really work.

11. **Make a commitment** – Making a contract with yourself to complete something can get you in the mindset to conquer it. Try an online version like those on stickk.com.

12. **Consider hurdles** – It's not enough to dream of the ideal life as positive visualisations can make you feel like you've already achieved your goals and balk at obstacles you encounter in reality. So picture the hurdles you may hit and plan how to overcome them. Think about the good outcomes of achieving your goals, not just living the good life.

13. **Engage in doublethink** – Identify two major benefits of achieving your goal, then identify two major obstacles that may hold you back. Mull over each benefit and obstacle in turn.

14. **List resources and achievements** – Listing your available resources and achievements will shift your perceptions about your ability to achieve a goal or execute a task.

15. **Build in some slack** – Building a little leeway into your plans helps them feel more achievable. Importantly, it also makes it easier to get back on track when you slip up.

BUILDING HABITS SUCCESSFULLY

16. **Change one habit at a time** – Changing fewer habits at one time leads to better results. Select just one new habit and focus on that. Avoid adding on another habit until the first one has become a natural part of your routine.

17. **Pick a valuable habit** – Choose the habit that will reap the biggest rewards in your life. For example, an exercise habit may benefit your productivity, sleep, nutrition, and energy.

18. **Make it easy** – When beginning a habit, make it as mindlessly easy as possible. For example, you could decide to only perform the habit for a maximum of two minutes a day, until you have established the pattern of performing it regularly. This will help you avoid feeling overwhelmed as you install your habit.

19. **Design your day** – List all the activities you do during the day and indicate if they are positive (e.g. exercising), negative (e.g. using social media) or neutral (e.g. brushing your teeth). Then, consider how you can redesign your day to cut out negative behaviours and tie in positive habits with your existing routine.

20. **Connect new and old habits** – Connect the new habits you wish to adopt with the habits that you already perform in order to create a habit chain where the old habit acts as a trigger for the new one. This will make it easier to stick with your new habit.

21. **Make it desirable** – Pair the habit you want to build with something you love to do, e.g. only watch your favourite TV show while using the treadmill.

22. **Specify day, time, and location** – When you are introducing a new habit into your life, your chances of success will double if you specifically plan and write down on which day, at what time, and in what location you will execute the activity. That's a major boost to your chances, so make a specific plan right away!

23. **Adopt the if/then format** – The 'if/then' format is a great way to use a trigger to form a good habit, e.g. If it is 7 am, then I'll meditate for 10 minutes. Habits replace willpower which is an exhaustible resource.

24. **Create a social contract** – Make a written, signed contract with a friend that if you do not act on your habit execution plan, you will give them a sum of money, donate to an institution you hate, or perform an embarrassing act. Ask them to follow up and hold you accountable.

25. **Automate your habits** – Where possible, make a habit the automatic default – for example by automatically routing a part of your salary to a savings account every month, or deleting your social media apps so that mindless browsing is no longer an option.

26. **Design the environment** – Shape the environment to make it easier to meet your goal – hide temptations and distractions (close tabs, pause your inbox, allocate time to attend to other matters), and place supportive resources in prominent places.

27. **Match environments to habits** – Avoid using the same location to execute both desirable and undesirable habits as that makes it easy to slide into doing the more convenient habit. This could mean using different web browsers for work and play or different seating options for different activities (e.g. chair versus couch).

28. **Take frequent action** – How frequently you perform an action (e.g. every day at 4 pm) matters more towards ingraining it as a habit than the duration of time you strive to perform it (e.g. occasionally over a four-week period). Take action regularly to install a new habit.

29. **Time it right** – Ask yourself when you are realistically most likely to be successful at following through on your habit, and plan accordingly. For example, if it's not practical to perform your meditation habit first thing in the morning, plan to do it at a time that is more feasible for you.

30. **Create a cue** – Set up a trigger to remind you to execute your habit. This could be a simple notification on your phone or strategically placing an object that reminds you to perform your habit in a place where you cannot miss it.

OVERCOMING PROCRASTINATION

31. **Break it down** – Break down what you need to do into manageable chunks you can tackle daily. Making a task less overwhelming will make it easier for you to complete it.

32. **Consider regret** – When you feel the urge to procrastinate, think about how much you would regret not doing the thing you seek to do.

33. **Ask whom it might help** – Think about a person who will benefit from the work you are doing as this can be a powerful motivator.

34. **Recall past successes** – Boost positivity and confidence by thinking back to an instance when you did well on a similar task.

35. **Find a friend** – Doing things with friends makes goals seem much more surmountable. Even thinking about a friend helps! Those who mail friends about their progress in quitting smoking, dieting, exercise, etc. do a much better job of sticking to goals.

36. **Find a competitor** – Having a competitor can boost performance and goal achievement. For example, compete with your partner or colleague to see who can clock more miles on a run.

37. **Keep a journal** – People who keep a journal of their ambitions are about 30% more likely to achieve them a reality.

38. **Escape temptations** – If you feel tempted to procrastinate, label your negative emotions to create distance from them, introduce a competing goal (like pride in your self-control) and distract yourself or wait out your emotional spike.

39. **Pull it close** – When you physically pull something closer, it makes it more interesting to you. For more interest in

your meeting or project, pull the table or your laptop nearer.

40. **Power pose** – Strike a powerful pose (think Wonder Woman or Superman) when you need a boost of confidence before a big task.

41. **Make a fist or cross your arms** – Simply clenching your fists or crossing your arms can boost your willpower and improve perseverance.

42. **Use loss aversion** – People hate to lose things more than they love to gain things, so tie your milestones to consequences, e.g. if you don't act on a task, plan to give out a sum of money or do 20 push-ups.

43. **Get started** – Human brains are wired to want to finish what is started, so the next time you're procrastinating, commit to working for just 5 minutes, and let your eager brain take over!

44. **Stop midway** – Stop midway through a task with a clear next step. It will create a powerful open loop that will motivate you to return to finish. Try halting your writing mid-sentence.

45. **Check it off** – As you complete a task, check it off with a satisfyingly big tick or crossed out mark, or on an app that pings. This will give you a mental 'right on!'

46. **Use music to motivate** – Songs with heavy bass (think hard rock or hip hop) can make you feel more powerful. Create a motivational playlist.

47. **Make a mantra** – Tell yourself out loud that what you're doing is important and achievable, it can increase your motivation.

48. **Set up small wins** – Celebrate mini milestones on the journey towards your goals with small treats as it will boost motivation and productivity.

49. **Consider abstaining** – When trying to kick a bad habit, consider that abstaining entirely can sometimes be easier than aiming for moderation as an experience can trigger further temptation.

50. **Jot down daily wins** – A Harvard study found daily journaling about small successes boosts creativity and motivation. Recording your progress, plans, benefits, and rewards (in any format) boosts perseverance. Cap off your workday by writing down what you've accomplished.

51. **Be a little behind** – Believing you are a little behind time or a little behind the competition is more motivating than believing you are very much behind or even a little ahead.

52. **Start a chain** – Track your success in meeting a daily target visually on a calendar. Your brain won't want to break the success chain.

13

Productivity

"If we did the things we are capable of,
we would astound ourselves."
Thomas Edison

Given that we have limited years of life during which to achieve our goals, it makes sense to try to extract the most value from our time. The following practices can help you maximise your productivity - and perhaps get you that much closer to your goals.

SETTING UP FOR PRODUCTIVITY

1. **Make your bed** – Doing this first thing right, first thing in the morning can set you up mentally for a productive day ahead.

2. **Meditate** – Participants in a study who meditated daily for three months enjoyed an increased ability to pay attention and those who kept at it saw improvements for seven years after the initial training!

3. **Benefit from nature** – Memory and attention improved 20% after people spent an hour in nature. Meanwhile, the colour green boosts creativity.

4. **Start with exercise** – Walking clears your brain, improves concentration, and induces creativity.

5. **Get happy** – Your brain in a positive state is 31% more productive than your brain in a negative, neutral, or stressed state. Make a list of mood boosters to enjoy before you start a task.

6. **Silence your phone** – You already knew it, but science also says the constant pinging of your phone is hurting your productivity. At the very least, disable notifications.

7. **Batch email checking** – Allocate two times a day to check your email. Use the rest of the day to focus on your most important tasks without the distraction of a pinging inbox. Tools like 'Freedom' can schedule when your email reaches your inbox.

8. **Retain control of your schedule** – Intentionally respond slowly to email and messages. Don't let other people dictate how you will spend your time. Let your correspondence work to your schedule rather than the other way around.

9. **Clean up your desk** – A clear desk will give you greater clarity of mind. Similarly, clean up your computer

desktop, close those tabs and search for 'unsubscribe' in your email to get rid of all those unwanted e-newsletters.

10. **Lift your laptop** – Those who hunch are less able to persevere at problems. So place the centre of your screen slightly above your eye line to boost your productivity.

11. **Dress right** – Your attire can prime your attitude. A business blazer can make you feel more powerful and effective and quirky outfits can make you feel more creative.

12. **Create a soundtrack** – Use the power of psychology to prime your brain for certain activities. Simply play the same song each time you perform a particular activity – and only then. This will train your brain to associate the music with the activity and help to get you in the zone!

13. **Choose your tools** – Rather than adopting any tool, identify the most important things in your life, and adopt tools that help you further those things in meaningful ways.

14. **Schedule your priorities** – Check if the items on your schedule are aligned with your goals. As Stephen Covey said, "The key is not to prioritise what's on your schedule, but to schedule your priorities."

15. **Eat well** – Employees eating 5+ servings of fruits and veggies at least 4 times a week are 20% more productive. Avoid soft drinks, fast food, sweets, cereal, white bread, and pasta. Opt for eggs, bananas, yoghurt, and blueberries for breakfast, and leafy greens, avocados,

almonds, olive oil, salads, salmon, brown rice, broccoli, and eggplant for lunch and dinner.

16. **Snack healthy** – Snack on fruits and veggies, carrots, walnuts, cashews, and dark chocolate.

17. **Enjoy your tea** – Those who relax with a cup of tea demonstrate more creativity than those who do not.

18. **Try ambient sounds** – Being in environments with light background sounds like birdsong or the chatter of a coffee shop can actually boost your focus. Visit a park or coffee shop to work, or try a website that imitates such sounds.

19. **Find a view** – Can't get outside? Even looking outside helps!

20. **Green your space** – Exposure to the colour green makes people happier, less tired, and more motivated. Try updating your curtains or lampshade.

21. **Set the temperature** – Set a comfortable temperature as your productivity will take a hit if you feel too warm or too cold. 22°C (72°F) is supposed to be a sweet spot.

22. **Look at puppies** – Yes, puppies! Looking at pictures of cute animals can boost your productivity. Cute cat videos work too.

23. **Nurture plants** – Simply having a plant on your desk can lower stress and improve attention and creativity.

24. **Hide the clock** – If you want to focus on or engage with an activity, hide the clock. You will be less engaged when focusing on the time it takes to do something.

25. **Do a pre-mortem** – Before you start a new project, imagine the worst possible outcome and consider exactly what might make it occur – then plan how you will ensure it does not take place.

26. **Practice conscientiousness** – Of the 'Big Five' personality traits, conscientiousness most determines success. So, act conscientiously. Make your bed. Be on time. Follow through.

27. **Act creative** – To become more creative, act like you are creative. Doodle, draw, paint, or sculpt!

28. **Have diverse interests** – Nobel Laureates have significantly more and deeper interests than average scientists. Exploring many interests deeply will fuel your overall thinking quality and creativity.

29. **Leverage tiredness** – People are typically most creative when groggy, so make use of tiredness for writing and ideation.

30. **Develop a winner mentality** – Imagining you've already won and are performing to keep your win is more effective than believing you're pursuing what you never had. Picturing yourself at peak performance creates neural pathways that make the actual task easier.

31. **Feel lucky** – People who engage in good luck rituals or carry good luck charms often get a boost of confidence that actually helps them perform better.

ADOPTING A PRODUCTIVE PROCESS

32. **Focus on process** – Focusing on the process to meet a goal rather than the outcome leads to better results. What steps do you need to take to meet your goal?

33. **Establish a foolproof process** – 76% of those who followed the following 5 steps accomplished their goals or were halfway there: 1) Write down your goals for the next 4 weeks; 2) Rate each goal on difficulty, importance, your commitment, whether you have the skills, and whether you've tried it before and succeeded; 3) List your action commitments for each goal; 4) Share these with a friend; 5) Send weekly progress reports to that friend.

34. **Select one primary task** – List out, in order of priority, the elements of your life that you wish to devote your attention to. To make sure you spend each day meaningfully, based on this list, select and schedule a single task every day which, once done, would make that day a success. Consider an urgent, important or fulfilling mid-sized task that would take about 60-90 minutes.

35. **Set three goals** – Don't set too many goals per day as this could turn out to be demotivating. Limit yourself to three small goals that contribute to your larger goal and then get cracking on each one in turn.

36. **Create stakes** – For the ultimate motivation, up the stakes by scheduling a time in the future to display your work. Tell your boss when to expect your project, sign up to do an exhibition at a gallery, or invite your friends over on a future date to eat the meal you're learning to cook.

37. **Halve the deadline** – Often the time to complete a job expands to fit the time available. Halving the deadline can create greater motivation to get things done.

38. **Use a checklist** – Checklists have an impressive impact on effectiveness – in hospitals, they even save lives. Use them often, particularly in the afternoons when alertness levels take a dip.

39. **Do the biggest task first** – Do your biggest task first and it won't bog you down; the rest of your day will seem a breeze.

40. **Single-task** – Focus on one task at a time. Multitasking does not work and drains cognitive resources. It is like saying "A1, B2, C3, D4" rather than the smoother "A, B, C, D and 1, 2, 3, 4".

41. **Batch similar tasks** – Doing similar tasks consecutively can help you make use of the similar mindset they require.

42. **Apply the 2-min rule** – If a task will take less than two minutes, do it immediately. You can take 2 minutes!

43. **Make time visible** – Purchase a gadget called a 'Time Timer' which provides a visual indication of the time remaining for a task by displaying a gradually disappearing coloured disk. The physical representation of time helps boost productivity. Alternatively, try the Time Timer mobile app.

44. **Draft it first** – Churn out an imperfect first draft without too much attention to missing pieces. Returning to fill in

the gaps is more productive than trying to make it perfect all at once.

45. **Prioritise** – Remember, it's common for 80% of results to come from 20% of work. Ask yourself if every activity on your plate will help you reach a goal – if not, eliminate it.

46. **Delegate** – If something can be done 80% as well by someone else, you are better off delegating it. Ask yourself how long it would take a smart college graduate to learn how to do it on your behalf.

47. **Embrace restrictions** – Avoid stressing about the limitations placed on you. People with more constraints (e.g. less budget) often produce more creative output.

48. **Follow up** – Create a 'waiting for' list sorted by emails, phone calls, money owed, etc. to ensure inactive items don't go forgotten.

49. **Aim to improve** – Instead of just practicing regularly, practice with the intention to improve. Track your failings and your success in correcting them with each practice run – it is the fastest way to improve.

50. **Talk to yourself** – Did you know that talking to yourself out loud in the second person ("you"/"your") can help you perform challenging tasks better?

51. **Ask 5 why's** – To find out what is holding you back, try asking the question 'why' 5 times to get at the root cause. It is a simple way to pierce through the multiple layers of an issue.

USING ENERGY TO YOUR ADVANTAGE

52. **Capture energy** – Energy levels naturally fluctuate throughout the day so track your peak energy periods and do your most important work accordingly.

53. **Recognise energy dips** – Be vigilant about the fact that you will be less alert and agreeable when your energy is off-peak (typically around 2-3 pm), and plan less-important tasks for this time. 2.55 pm is supposed to be the most unproductive time of the day.

54. **Make coffee work for you** – Drink coffee half an hour before your usual energy dips. If you use it when you're already tired, it's too late. Don't know your usual energy dips? Simply track your energy level from hour to hour over a few days to spot the pattern.

55. **Employ an energy trigger** – Make use of your existing energy triggers, e.g. if high-energy songs get you grooving, play them for a boost.

56. **Activate human energy boosters** – Make a list of people who make you feel energised and meet or call them whenever you need an energy boost.

MAKING THE MOST OF BREAKS

57. **Plan regular breaks** – Breaks improve productivity, decision-making, and creativity, more so than the number of hours put in. A good break involves no heavy thinking and is even better if it includes some socialising,

movement, meditation, or best of all, time in nature. Take a 15-minute break every hour.

58. **Take walking breaks** – Standing and walking for 5 mins every hour during the workday boosts productivity.

59. **Walk creative** – Walking in meandering, fluid patterns helps you generate more creative ideas than walking in straight and boxy patterns.

60. **Seek social breaks** – Social breaks provide a productivity boost.

61. **Watch dog videos** – Yes, there's scientific evidence of the replenishing effects of watching dog videos!

62. **Daydream** – Daydreaming actually boosts creativity, so let your mind wander.

63. **Do something else** – To inspire creativity, step away from the task you're working on, and work on something else for a while, like a puzzle.

IMPROVING DECISION MAKING

64. **Avoid decision fatigue** – Even minor decision making is cognitively draining, so automate and streamline small decisions like what to eat and wear, so you have the mental bandwidth for the big stuff. Don't dwell on small choices – set a timer for 3 minutes to decide.

65. **Decide for others** – People typically make better decisions for others than themselves. So when you have a tough choice to make, consider how you'd advise a friend in your place.

66. **Look for alternatives** – The best decisions are made by those who take time to look for and evaluate many different options rather than treating a single option as black or white.

67. **Exempt minor choices** – With minor choices (like which sauce to buy), too many options create choice fatigue. So instead of wasting time evaluating, settle on 'good enough'.

68. **Flip a coin** – When you can't choose between two options, flip a coin! Because while it's in the air, you may get a better sense of which way your intuition wants it to land. If you still can't decide, make a pro/con list to evaluate the benefits and consequences of the various options.

14
Leadership

"I alone cannot change the world, but I can cast a stone across the water to create many ripples."
Mother Teresa

Leading other people is no easy task. Taking on or being bestowed with a leadership role doesn't automatically equip us with the skills we need to perform that role effectively. The following research summarises the best practices of the most effective leaders.

SETTING THE STAGE FOR HIGH PERFORMANCE

1. **Prepare the workspace** – Adjustable standing desks, open windows, enclosed private offices, and personalised workspaces all boost productivity. High

ceilings, dimmer lighting, messy desks, and some light background noise promote creative, abstract thinking.

2. **Provide the tools** – Having the materials and equipment they need to do their work right is a major driver of employee satisfaction and performance.

3. **Communicate end goals** – Efficiency increases when employees know the end goal of their work.

4. **Motivate with meaning** – Give employees meaning by encouraging customers to talk to them about the impact the products make on their lives, and helping staff curate charitable projects. Working for a good cause can boost productivity by up to 30%.

5. **Promote standards over rules** – Promote standards such as Southwest Airlines' guide to "Create fun for customers". Cut down on the rules – Google's dress code is: "You must wear clothes".

6. **Prioritise work by customer needs** – Ensure customers' accuracy needs are met first, then work to provide greater availability, partnership, and advice.

7. **Define measurable outcomes, not methods** – Specifying the outcomes you want creates positive tension, but allow employees to get creative in how they meet those outcomes. Make all outcomes measurable (you should be able to count, rate, or rank them).

8. **Plan performance** – Meet at an interval which the employee finds comfortable to ask them about actions taken, discoveries made and partnerships built and discuss performance accordingly. After 10 minutes, ask

about the actions, discoveries, and partnerships planned for the future and refer to these at the next performance planning meeting.

9. **Learn from your best** – Starting with the most significant roles, revise all training to learn from the best practices of your best-performing employees.

10. **Set realistic timelines** – Use real-life experience to gauge how long a project is realistically likely to take, as people have a strong tendency to underestimate this, particularly when they are working in groups.

PRACTICING POSITIVE LEADERSHIP

11. **Be optimistic** – Optimistic leaders create more engaged and productive employees.

12. **Show empathy** – Empathic bosses see better results from their team as employees trust them to look after their interests.

13. **Choose questions over instructions** – Ask questions rather than give instructions, e.g. "Would you please do XYZ?"

14. **Tell stories** – Stories foster a sense of belonging. Even stories of failure and vulnerability work.

15. **Impart power** – Signal to your reports that you want them to take on authority. Do interviews in panels. Make committee decisions. Relinquish control whenever possible.

16. **Give trust** – Giving trust readily will improve performance. If an employee breaks your trust, view it as the exception, not the rule.

17. **Boost positive interactions** – 3:1 is the ratio of positive to negative interactions that make for a positive work environment. However, a ratio of 6:1 is ideal.

18. **Spend time with stars** – Give the most time to your best people as they deserve your attention. Managers typically do the opposite, spending the most time with weak performers.

19. **Reply emails** – The longer a boss takes to reply email, the less satisfied his or her team tends to be with their leadership.

20. **Invite alternate views** – Encourage everyone to adopt an alternate perspective. Ask "What might we be missing? If we did this completely differently how should we do it?"

21. **Ask to be challenged** – Encourage your team to tell you when you are wrong. Criticise yourself. Ask for feedback. Say 'Here's a dopey idea' to encourage people to challenge you. Celebrate those who challenge you and reward their candour by making changes fast.

22. **Manage your bad days** – Tell your team when you're having a bad day and let them know that if you're grouchy, it's not because of them. Otherwise, your mood will be contagious.

RECRUITING RIGHT

23. **Don't expect personality changes** – When recruiting and training, acknowledge that skills can be learned and knowledge given, but personality (what motivates people, how they think and relate to others) is heavily determined in childhood and adolescence and virtually unchangeable.

24. **Interview right** – Know the motivations, thinking and relating styles of top performers in the role (both inside and outside your organisation) and ask open-ended questions that gauge whether prospective employees have those characteristics.

25. **Test for grit** – Grit or perseverance has a huge bearing on success in any role so consider testing prospective recruits for grit. You can find a template test online.

26. **Evaluate empathy** – Members of the highest performing teams score above average for empathy. Try an empathy test which gauges social sensitivity by asking participants to determine thoughts and feelings based on photographs of people's eyes. Women typically score higher than men.

27. **Get to know recruits** – Ask recruits about their professional (and even personal) goals, their preferred styles of receiving recognition (private or public), and how they learn best from others. Strive to find something you like in every employee and to care for them.

OPTIMISING TEAMWORK

28. **Foster team belonging** – Teams operate best when they have a sense of belonging, which can be fostered with similar clothing, friendly touches (be sure to consider appropriateness), and working in sync.

29. **Promote unison** – If you want people to bond, get them to act in unison, and collaborate. Teams that eat together produce more. Even singing together works.

30. **Get close to collaborate** – Those whose workspaces are physically close collaborate far more.

31. **Skip brainstorming** – Generating ideas alone produces more and better ideas than group brainstorming.

32. **Mix thinking styles** – Teaming up those who think differently from one another boosts creative output.

33. **Understand team motivation** – Motivation in teams tends to start getting activated halfway towards the deadline.

34. **Share ideas early, coach later** – Teams generally become less open to new ideas after the mid-point of a project, but they also become more open to coaching.

35. **Cater to team commitment** – When team commitment is high is a good time to emphasise what has to be done. When team commitment is low, it's better to highlight progress already made, even if it isn't very significant.

36. **Selectively leverage competition** – Competition tends to make teams of men more creative but teams of women less so.

37. **Resolve conflict collaboratively** – If people have issues with each other, don't listen to one gripe alone to you. Ask them to try to speak directly to that person, and if that doesn't work out, offer to be a part of a three-way conversation.

RECOGNISING AND REWARDING

38. **Recognise weekly** – Provide specific praise and recognition for good work at least once a week. When you start a meeting by praising a team member's success, it can raise the performance of the whole group by a remarkable 31%.
39. **Choose rewards carefully** – Rewards are less important than intrinsic satisfaction and social support and large monetary rewards can even negatively impact the intrinsic pleasure people get from their work.
40. **Reward process over outcome** – Reward a good process and the outcome will take care of itself. Shape behaviour by rewarding even small improvements.
41. **Offer relevant rewards** – Match the way you reward employees with their personalities and what best motivates them.
42. **Share equal prestige** – Create heroes in every role by acknowledging excellence at every level. Give public recognition, bright titles, and the capacity to earn double what an average performer would get in every role.

43. **Broadband salary scales** – Broadband salary scales for different roles. For example, the top bracket for an excellent waiter could be higher than the bottom bracket for a mediocre restaurant manager. So someone just promoted to restaurant manager could actually get a salary cut until they show excellence in their new role, after which they could earn more.

44. **Conduct regular reviews** – Hold semi-annual (e.g. quarterly) rather than annual one-on-one performance meetings where you discuss the employee's performance (against measurable outcomes) for 10 minutes, then focus on his/her goals for the coming months, how these could be measured, how best to achieve them, and how you can help.

45. **Celebrate personal bests** – Allow employees to assess their own progress monthly or quarterly and compete with themselves.

46. **Help employees ascend** – Ensure a personality fit with a new role (consider motivations, thinking style, and relating style) before promoting an employee, and allow them to return to the previous role if they aren't able to perform in the new one.

47. **Don't promise a bonus** – Promising employees a bonus to achieve better results actually makes them perform worse! Instead offer non-monetary celebrations like pizza or a note of thanks which create lasting increases in productivity.

48. **Avoid corporate awards** – Corporate awards programs don't work as those who weren't awarded feel demotivated.

49. **Don't glorify failure** – Instead, recognise and repeat successes. Find the repeatable pattern.

ADDRESSING PERFORMANCE ISSUES

50. **Give feedback immediately** – Don't procrastinate giving feedback. Only wait if the person is hungry, angry, or tired. Deliver negative feedback in person, privately, and focus on the behaviour, not the person. Don't wait for a performance review – you don't use going to the dentist annually as a reason not to brush your teeth daily.

51. **Abstain from using power** – Using power to get your own way damages relationships and camaraderie. It communicates that you care only about your own goals. You move from respected partner to feared enforcer.

52. **Evaluate a lack of motivation** – Consider why a person may not be motivated. Is what they ought to do hard or boring? Are others encouraging them not to do it? Is the task at odds with what they're being rewarded for? If the activity is somehow undesirable, try to help.

53. **Share natural consequences** – Describe what problems the negative behaviour naturally creates for the person, for you, and others, and what might happen if it continues, e.g. "I know it's a hassle but it could affect your

reputation in the company unless it's done." Connect to his or her values.

54. **Highlight long-term benefits** – Describe the potential future benefits of new behaviour. When you believe they agree on what needs to be done, stop – avoid overselling.

55. **Explain coping mechanisms** – If a person refuses to comply, explain the workaround you'll adopt, e.g. "I can't give you critical path assignments if I can't be sure you'll get them done."

56. **Be an enabler and supporter** – If the person lacks ability, help by removing any barriers to getting work done. Do they lack skills or knowledge? Are others withholding information or material? Ask if you are somehow adding to the problem. Ask about systems, work layout, policies, procedures. Ask "If you ran this place, what would you do to solve this problem?" Get at the root cause of the issue by asking 'why' five times.

57. **Solve it jointly** – Ask "What do you think it'll take to fix this?" Engaging the other person's involvement to help solve the issue will boost their commitment.

58. **Look for a long-term solution** – Seek a solution that would solve the problem for everyone rather than a one-time fix. Do away with bureaucratic hindrances. Can the workspace or procedure change? Could technology, gadgets or data help?

59. **Address miscasting** – If weak performance is due to a personality misfit against the role, there are three options: Create a system to support them in solving the issue (e.g.

a checklist), find a complementary partner for them, or find an alternate role for them.

60. **Resolve emerging problems first** – During the discussion, if a new problem emerges that needs immediate attention (e.g. a lie, insubordination, a decision made without consultation, etc.), clarify that you need to address this. Place a bookmark where you just were and resolve the new problem before returning to the original issue.

61. **Make a plan** – Establish who (one person) needs to do precisely what (be very specific on this) and by when exactly (date and time) and decide how and when to follow up based on risk (how risky/crucial is the project?), trust (what is the person's track record?), and competence (how experienced is the person in the area?).

62. **Provide discipline as needed** – Know the formal processes and deliver discipline somberly. Explain the next level of discipline if the behaviour continues, and follow through as you describe.

63. **Avoid delaying termination** – If performance hovers around average with no upward trend, don't wait too long to move on. Use language like: "This isn't a fit for you, let's talk about why" or "We need to find a role that plays more to your natural strengths, what do you think that role might be?" Don't blame the person, ill performance is simply an issue of miscasting.

15

Persuasion

"In a gentle way, you can shake the world."
Mahatma Gandhi

Often in life, to achieve our goals, we need to convince other people to come around to our way of thinking. The following practices can help you secure the buy-in you need to successfully introduce ideas and initiate a change of hearts and minds. Use them for good.

COMMUNICATING CONVINCINGLY

1. **Start small** – Be a tempered radical. Instead of bludgeoning people over the head with hard-to-stomach ideas, use a Trojan Horse. Make it look more innocent and build buy-in.

2. **Highlight shared goals** – Facts don't convince people. Instead, highlight shared goals and showcase your similarities to your audience so they'll be open to listening.

3. **Connect to what they know** – Make ideas more appealing by connecting them with ideas that are already well understood by the audience.

4. **Add a 'because'** – Giving a brief reason makes it feel like you're making a request rather than forcing your opinion. It doesn't matter much what the reason is, more that you had one.

5. **Share individual impact** – People are far more moved by the impact on specific individuals whom they are made to relate with rather than large numbers of people who can seem abstract and unfamiliar.

6. **Point out negatives** – Cultivate credibility by highlighting the reasons not to support your idea. This can actually encourage buy-in.

7. **Communicate expressively** – Smiling, modulating your speech, minimising pauses, and varying your pitch, tone and volume will make you come across as more knowledgeable, intelligent, and thoughtful.

8. **Nod as you speak** – If you want someone to agree with you, nod as you speak. Humans are naturally wired to mirror the actions of those they look at.

9. **Present testable ideas** – Present ideas that others can test for themselves practically, as these are far more convincing.

10. **Make it familiar** – Reactions to ideas get more positive after 10-20 exposures to the idea, especially if they're short, spaced apart by a few days, and mixed in with other ideas.

11. **Remind them of their support** – Remind people of times they acted in favour of what you want them to support rather than when they didn't and they will have a stronger belief in the cause.

12. **Get them saying yes** – People like to be consistent. Get them saying yes early on and they will keep at it.

13. **Use the power of reciprocation** – Small favours, when they seem genuine, encourage people to reciprocate. The effect is greater when it occurs between strangers and favours are small but thoughtful. But the impact wears with time so request your return favour soon afterwards.

14. **Employ positive peer pressure** – People are more likely to do virtually anything when they know that many others are doing the same.

15. **Impart information** – Make the impact of choices tangible at the point of decision making. For example, if you want people to use the cheap gloves for small jobs rather than the expensive ones, display the prices of the gloves prominently on the glove boxes.

16. **Provide a map** – If you want people to visit a particular place, give them a map (even if the place is easy to find) as it increases the likelihood they will actually go there.

17. **Use a graph** – Simply using a graph to communicate the same information can increase its credibility from 67% to 96%!

18. **Request small favours** – People will think they like you if they see themselves doing something for you, and then be more open to your ideas.

19. **Ask for clarity** – To expose gaps in a person's knowledge, simply ask them for detailed explanations. They will often come to realise they aren't as savvy as they thought.

20. **Find an ally** – Find one person who believes in your vision and make them your ally. Having a partner boosts performance.

DESIGNING A PERSUASIVE PITCH

21. **Get your order right** – If you are competing with others, aim to start first if you are up against strong contenders, up against few contenders, or not the default choice. Also, if you are being listed on a ballot. If there are many contenders or the other contenders are weak, aim to present last to stand out.

22. **Do something different** – Ask yourself "Are people going to feel like telling someone else what I told them?" Make people sit up, e.g. change your introduction from the usual template, use a whiteboard rather than PowerPoint.

23. **Practice your pitch** – Run your pitch by peers before the actual delivery. This will help you build confidence and bridge gaps.

24. **Dress smart** – To be more persuasive, whether in business or romance, dress professionally (think suit/tie). Keep in mind that showing more skin makes you appear less intelligent as it distracts attention from your mind. Also, wear your glasses – you'll be seen as more intelligent.

25. **Demonstrate authority** – Signal what makes you a credible, knowledgeable authority before you make your influence attempt. Do this with your attire, certificates, recommendations, etc.

26. **Be likeable** – People are better influenced by those whom they like. And they typically like those who are similar to them, who compliment them, and who cooperate with them in realising goals.

27. **Use your middle initial** – Using your middle initial creates a positive impression of your intellect and abilities. Be sure to include it on your CV and work reports.

28. **Seat them softly** – Soft furniture promotes agreeable behaviour while hard furniture has the opposite effect.

29. **Keep them warm** – Warm drinks promote agreement, so opt to serve a warm drink over a cool one.

30. **Orchestrate a pull** – When people physically pull something closer, it becomes more desirable to them.

Slide your proposal to your client so they have to pull it close to examine it.

31. **Make it the default option** – Ask if clients want to pay by card or with cash (which assumes they are okay to buy) or say, "If I don't hear back from you by the end of the day, I'll assume you are okay with the proposal."

32. **Make it scarce** – People are wired to place a higher value on things that are harder to obtain. Create scarcity and you will increase desire.

INITIATING A CHANGE MOVEMENT

33. **Identify key behaviours** – Start by identifying the key behaviours which, if changed, will make the biggest difference. Be specific about the desired alternate behaviours.

34. **Prescribe recovery behaviours** – Know what actions need to take place to recover in the event a problem does occur.

35. **Change others' behaviour** – Both motivation and ability matter. Convince them that it is, one, worth it and, two, that they can do it.

36. **Communicate effectively** – If you're proposing a comfortable change, highlight the benefits of change. If it's a risky change, highlight the instability of the current situation, clearly connecting the current behaviour and expected negative outcome. Offer hope by showing specifically how to solve the problem.

37. **Create a sense of urgency** – A sense of urgency is the factor that generates the most buy-in in change initiatives.

38. **Provide experiences** – Personal experience goes further than words when it comes to changing behaviour. Try to help people experience the difference themselves. Encourage them to try out an activity – they may find they like it.

39. **Tell vivid stories** – Use real-world stories that people can imagine themselves experiencing to activate emotion and change behaviour. Take your time to play the story out, don't cut to the chase – make it plot-twisting and emotive.

40. **Surrender control** – Help people figure out what they want. Use empathy, ask questions, listen, and help them examine how they can live according to their values. People can make enormous sacrifices when their actions are anchored in their own values.

41. **Make it easy** – Where possible, make change easy by making the difficult easy, the averse pleasant, and the boring interesting.

42. **Build social capital** – When striving to create change, get positive people on your side before you even attempt to convert the negative ones. This will allow you to build valuable social capital that will make all the difference.

43. **Find the influencers** – The message is no more important than the messenger, so identify respected influencers and spend disproportionate time with them.

Present data that helps them understand the problem, listen to their concerns, build trust with them, be open to their ideas, and rely on them.

44. **Be an opinion leader** – Be seen as knowledgeable (by staying connected with the field), trustworthy (by using your knowledge to help), and generous with your time (by having frequent positive interactions with others).

45. **Build capability** – Foster ability with deliberate practice (even for activities like interpersonal interactions). Ask people to track what they're doing, what's working, what isn't, and why, study best practices, and focus on improving their behaviours (rather than outcomes). Treat setbacks as chances to learn what doesn't work.

46. **Make them advocates** – To make people believe something, get them to advocate for it. Asking people to wear badges or make statements, speeches, or posters supporting a view can make them ardent supporters of that view.

47. **Create a culture** – Make change the easiest option by shaping a new culture around the desired behaviours.

16
Giving

*"Those who bring sunshine to the lives of others
cannot keep it from themselves."*
James M. Barrie

Humans are altruistic by nature, and research shows that giving has an impressive impact on your own wellbeing and sense of abundance. Here are some practices for designing a more fulfilling life rich in giving.

GIVING IN CASH AND KIND

1. **Donate to charity** – In every major region of the world, people who give money to charity are happier than those who do not, even after taking into account their own personal financial situation. In fact, it has about the same impact on happiness as doubled income!

2. **Choose effective charities** – Maximise the good you do by helping in countries and places with the least resources (i.e. not the developed world), and selecting initiatives which provide the greatest reduction of suffering. Find charities that meet such criteria by visiting thelifeyoucansave.org.

3. **Give as much as you can** – Consider calculating the expenses you will need to lead a comfortable life and donating everything you earn over that.

4. **Make it automatic** – Setting up an automated system to make donations will make it that much easier.

5. **See your impact** – Contributing has a bigger boost on your happiness when the impact you make is more visible and tangible. Consider how you can contribute in a way in which you can see the outcome for yourself.

6. **Donate as you declutter** – Do a mock move! Donate everything you wouldn't take with you if you were moving house. Before you start decluttering, identify libraries and charities to which to donate the books, clothes, etc. you don't need.

7. **Share surplus food** – Instead of throwing away excess food, consider donating it or giving it to neighbours. Apps like Olio enable easy food sharing.

GIVING TIME

8. **Devote your career** – Seek out a career that can help you have the most positive impact on the world. The website 80000hours.org can help you with this.

9. **Volunteer** – 78% of volunteers say it lowers stress levels, 94% say it improves their mood, 96% say it enriches their sense of purpose and 25% say it helps them manage a chronic illness. Selfless volunteers actually live longer.

10. **Be a voluntourist** – Consider devoting a few days from your next vacation to give back to the community, whether it's working with children, the environment, or supporting economic projects.

GIVING LIFE

11. **Donate your organs and tissues posthumously** – One deceased organ donor can save up to eight lives! Meanwhile one tissue donor can benefit the lives of as many as 75 people.

12. **Donate your kidneys** – By donating a kidney as a living donor, you can give someone in need about 15 to 20 additional years of life.

13. **Donate blood** – Blood and platelets cannot be manufactured, they can only come from volunteer donors. One blood donation can potentially save up to three lives.

GIVING AS AN ORGANISATION

14. **Give via company initiatives** – When companies organise volunteer initiatives, employees are happier to work there, less stressed, and better in teamwork and time-management.

15. **Introduce opt-out schemes** – Suggest the company where you work introduces a policy where a portion (e.g. 1%) of every employee's salary is automatically donated to charity unless the employee actively opts out. People are much less likely to opt out due to human tendency to continue with the default option.

16. **Take the 1% pledge** – As a company, join the league of firms that have pledged to give 1% of equity, time, product, or profit to charity.

17. **Give a social bonus** – As an organisation, instead of giving a traditional bonus, consider allowing employees to donate a portion of their bonus to any charity they choose.

INSPIRING GIVING

18. **Share your actions** – Being open about your giving behaviour encourages those around you to give too. So don't try to be overmodest – talk about your actions.

19. **Donate your birthday** – Social media websites like Facebook allow you to request donations to a charity on your birthday.

20. **Activate youth** – Inspire youth with ideas for how they can do good via dosomething.org, the largest not-for-profit exclusively for young people and social change

21. **Cultivate a giving habit** – Encourage your kids to donate a portion of their pocket money to charity.

22. **Highlight individuals over masses** – It's easier to empathise with an individual than a crowd, so to boost contribution to a cause you support, illustrate the plight of one person, not thousands (or even two people).

23. **Preselect who'd benefit** – Telling potential donors that a beneficiary family has been selected results in more donations than telling them a family will be selected.

24. **Show high impact** – People are more likely to donate if they are told their contribution will benefit a greater proportion out of the total number of those in need, even if the absolute number of people they will benefit is fewer.

25. **Highlight others' contributions** – People are far more likely to do what they ought to (e.g. recycle) when told that most of their neighbours are already doing it.

26. **Encourage small donations** – To encourage more donations use wording that implies that even small donations are valid, e.g. 'Every penny helps'.

27. **Rouse emotion** – Emotionally roused people (e.g. those asked to think about babies) asked to donate to an individual in need gave twice as much as those in neutral emotional states.

28. **Promote self-reflection** – Prompting people to reflect on their good fortune tends to make them more willing to contribute to the common good.

29. **Highlight victims over perpetrators** – As Martin Luther King Jr. did in his speech, to prompt effective action, draw attention to the victims of injustice, not the perpetrators.

30. **Make experiences tangible** – Activate empathy by getting people to behave as though they were those in difficult circumstances, e.g. navigating a wheelchair, experiencing a refugee camp in virtual reality, or using technology to simulate impaired sight. Activating empathy boosts donations.

31. **Use a red donation box** – Using a red donation box can promote giving as the colour red suggests urgency.

32. **Match donations** – 85% of people say they are more likely to donate if their donations are matched.

Green living

"The most frugal or greenest product
is the one you didn't buy."
Joshua Becker

As humans, many of our actions generate serious environmental consequences that disturb the ecosystems we operate in, our health, and the lives of future generations. The following practices will help you reduce your own environmental impact while reaping both financial and emotional rewards.

MINIMISING WASTE

1. **Go vegan** – Did you know animal farming is a major contributor to deforestation and results in more greenhouse gas emissions than all forms of transport combined? That's why cutting out meat and dairy could

be the single biggest way to reduce environmental impact.

2. **Become a minimalist** – Use less stuff. Make like Marie Kondo and donate everything that doesn't spark joy in you.

3. **Carry a reuse kit** – Always carry your own reusable bags, bottle, serviette, straw, and utensils and avoid using single-use items. Remember, single-use items can take up to 450 years to biodegrade.

4. **Buy less and consciously** – If possible, avoid buying at all. Repair what's broken, use what you have, borrow, rent, swap or build. If you must buy, buy second-hand, recycled, refillable, locally made, natural, and/or organic items. Choose items without packaging. Avoid plastic and never buy PVC (polyvinyl chloride) and petroleum-based products or products with VOCs (volatile organic compounds). Use your money to vote for the type of world you want to live in.

5. **Minimise e-waste** – Choose rechargeable, refurbished electronics. Look after them well and avoid replacing them often. Select smaller devices and choose Energy Star certified ones (and use power management mode). Donate/sell your tech when you're done with it.

6. **Go paperless** – Adopt a digital lifestyle. Do everything online – from accounting and banking to receiving subscriptions, receipts and statements, to making payments and buying tickets. Avoid printing anything, and if you absolutely must, use recycled paper and print double-sided.

7. **Compost** – Get or make a compost bin. Placing a bin within 5 feet of the front door increases composting rates by 141%. Put in an equal amount of dry waste (leaves and twigs) and wet waste (grass clippings, vegetable waste). Bury new scraps in the middle of the pile, having chopped up big chunks. When you're on the go, use a reusable coffee cup or other container to bring your lunch scraps home to compost.

8. **Recycle** – Reduce waste sent to landfill. Separate your paper, plastic, glass, and aluminium waste and pop them into a recycling bin.

9. **Commute consciously** – Telecommute when possible, but otherwise, walking, cycling, public transport, and car-pooling are the best options for getting around. If you must use a car, opt for an electric vehicle or hybrid. If not, buy used. Minimise time spent idling (it consumes 5-8% of fuel). Use lower-grade octane fuel or biodiesel. Improve fuel efficiency by as much as 10% with regular vehicle maintenance. And wash your car at a professional car wash as they use far less water.

10. **Gift consciously** – Choose to give cash, vouchers, and experiences (tickets, vacations, lessons, and memberships) over physical gifts. Research reveals that experiences make people happier than things anyway. Select recycled gift cards and skip gift-wrapping altogether.

11. **Be an eco-traveller** – Travel locally, off-season, and in groups, and choose eco-hotels. Pack light but take your own toiletries and water bottle, and use permanent (not

paper) luggage tags. Also, use the same linens and towels during your stay, turn off your room lights and wash your clothes at home on return.

12. **Carbon offset your life** – Use an online calculator to calculate your carbon footprint from air travel, driving, and home energy use. Then purchase the appropriate amount of carbon credits.

GREEN SHOPPING

13. **Green choices are contagious** – Eco-friendly efforts can be contagious, so install those solar panels and buy that hybrid car!

14. **Request no bags** – Plastic bags take 20 years to biodegrade and kill off wildlife. Use your own reusable bag, directly put purchases in your handbag or backpack, or simply carry them in hand.

15. **Opt out of paper receipts** – Paper receipts are toxic, not recyclable, and usually thrown away. Ask for a digital receipt instead.

16. **Dress sustainably** – Buy fewer clothes. Adopt a 'capsule wardrobe'. Host a clothes swap with friends. When you must buy, look for secondhand, recycled, undyed, organic cotton items, without real fur.

17. **Do green grocery shopping** – Buy local, fresh, organic, loose, in bulk, and only what you'll use. Look for less (and biodegradable) packaging.

GREENING YOUR HOME

18. **Build a green home** – Select a site that would shorten your commute and ideally one with existing infrastructure, select bamboo flooring, and reflective/light-coloured roofing, ensure windows face north or south, and use porous pavement. Choose recycled materials for the roof, countertops, paint, fabrics, etc.

19. **Insulate** – To create energy efficiency, use insulated concrete wall panels and double-pane windows. Even closing the curtains can reduce energy needs by 25%.

20. **Run on solar** – Solar energy is lauded as an inexhaustible fuel source that is pollution-free. Install solar panels and a solar water heater.

21. **Change your bulbs** – Dust your light bulbs and, when they burn out, switch to compact fluorescent (CFL) bulbs which use 66% less energy. Use dimming controls, and use timers or sensors to easily switch off lights. Use natural lighting whenever possible.

22. **Avoid air conditioning** – Choose to use fans instead. If you must use air conditioning, use an Energy Star system, use it at higher temperatures to save energy, and tune it. In cold environments, try to reduce heating. Maintaining a constant temperature saves energy.

23. **Choose green furnishings** – Opt for used furniture. Buy a mattress that wasn't treated with chemicals. Select organic cotton or bamboo sheets, and opt for wool rather than polyester blankets. Plus, fill your home with houseplants to create clean air!

24. **Save energy in the kitchen** – Use Energy Star qualified appliances as they use 10-15% less energy. Choose microwaves over ovens – they consume 50% less energy. Keep them clean to maximise energy. Avoid preheating ovens and be sure to use both oven racks at the same time. Keep both oven and refrigerator doors closed – no peeking! And position your fridge in the shade with a 10cm gap behind it.

25. **Minimise food waste** – Use perishable items before they spoil, measure carefully when cooking and save leftovers, both at home and when you eat out. Store and serve food in/on glass or ceramic.

26. **Switch off and unplug** – Switch off unused electronics and unplug appliances, especially the TV. It could save you an entire month's energy bill each year!

27. **Wash clothes efficiently** – Choose a front-loading Energy Star washing machine over a top-loader and set warm wash and cold rinse cycles (this saves 90% of energy over using hot water only). Hang dry your clothes rather than using the dryer.

28. **Save water** – Turn off the tap when you scrub dishes, shave, and brush your teeth. Run full loads in your dishwasher. Install a low-flow, dual-flush toilet and flush fewer times per day (one less flush and you'll save 4.5 gallons). Aim for 5-minute showers with an aerated showerhead, not long baths. Also, fix leaks fast!

29. **Rent a room** – It reduces per capita emissions almost as much as converting to heat pumps or insulating.

WHAT'S NEXT?

I hope you enjoyed *Cheat Sheets for Life* and are excited and inspired to put this information into practice and start living your best life. Here are some ideas on what you can do next.

Download free resources and tools

 If you'd like to access resources that can help you put some of these key concepts into practice, like the free *Cheat Sheets for Life* Habit Planner, you can scan this code or visit www.cheatsheets.life/#resources.

Gift copies to friends and family

 If you think this book would benefit others and would like to order paperback or e-book copies for friends and family, you can do so via www.amazon.com/dp/B08TYQ4HH8 or by scanning this code.

Leave a rating and review

 If you would like to share your rating or review, simply use your phone to scan this code or visit www.amazon.com/dp/B08TYQ4HH8 and click the button that says "Write a customer review". I read every review.

BIBLIOGRAPHY

 Access links to every book, journal, course and article referenced in *Cheat Sheets for Life* by using your phone to scan this code or visiting www.cheatsheets.life/index.php/bibliography.

RECOMMENDED RESOURCES

Below are a few recommended resources for further data-driven exploration of subjects covered in this book.

Books

- On wellbeing: 'The As If Principle' by Richard Wiseman
- On productivity: 'Atomic Habits' by James Clear
- On interpersonal relations: 'Crucial Confrontations' by Kerry Patterson, Joseph Grenny, Ron McMillan and Al Switzler
- On leadership: 'First, Break All the Rules' by Marcus Buckingham and Curt Coffman
- On giving: 'Doing Good Better' by William MacAskill

Online courses

- On wellbeing: 'The Science of Wellbeing' by Yale University
- On parenting: 'Everyday Parenting' by Yale University

ABOUT THE AUTHOR

Ayesha S. Ratnayake (MBA, Chartered Marketer) has over 10 years of experience in marketing and management.

She has served as CEO, Director and Shareholder of a technology firm where she led the development of an enterprise software product. She has also served as Co-founder and Director of a marketing communications agency. She is a startup mentor and a mental health advocate.

Ayesha is a Sri Lankan based in Colombo, and was born in Suva, Fiji. She can be contacted at hi@cheatsheets.life.

ACKNOWLEDGEMENTS

A loving thank you to my parents, Ajith Ratnayake and Hiranthi Ratnayake – everything I am and do, I owe to you.

Mountains of gratitude go out to the erudite Nalini Rodrigo, who enthusiastically edited and proofread the book and whose many recommendations have made it infinitely better.

I am also deeply grateful to Dinuka Lankaloka, who patiently and good-naturedly helped me prepare the cover to meet myriad changing specifications.

Finally, thank you to all the friends and family who give me precious feedback and support. You give me wings.

BY THE SAME AUTHOR

Love Your Life Workbook

Design a life you love – using over one hundred time-tested techniques

The *Love Your Life Workbook* makes the advice of researchers, scientists, psychologists and physicians more accessible, affordable and actionable. So you can practice tried and tested techniques to create happiness and fulfilment. Follow the exercises to:

- Step into the shoes of your ideal self
- Declutter your mind – and your living space
- Formulate the state of 'flow'
- Find your 'ikigai' once and for all
- Perform a comprehensive digital detox
- Hack the habits you want the most
- Turn around your worst days
- Become a conversation virtuoso
- Manage confrontation like a pro
- Play the dating game to win
- And tap 100+ more exercises to unlock your life!

Whether you want to feel more joy every day or feel stronger in times of struggle, the *Love Your Life Workbook* will help you press the accelerator on your journey towards a life you love.

To claim your copy, scan the code or visit www.amazon.com/dp/B09Y5VVN48.

The Utopia Playbook

Join the journey to the planet's most impressive places – and crack the blueprint for a utopian world.

If you've ever wondered what it would take to build a perfect world, you're not alone. A utopia full of happiness, health and abundance might sound like a pipe dream. But, if you look closely enough, the world is already full of utopias. *The Utopia Playbook* explores the countries that top the world's indices in all the metrics that matter. Tap the secrets of:

- Finland, which is the world's happiest country
- Hong Kong, which has the longest life expectancy
- Bhutan, which is carbon neutral
- Spain, which is the biggest organ donor
- France, which has the least food waste
- And dozens more countries that hold the keys to an ideal world

Discover where people can safely leave their babies in strollers by the street and which nation has doubled its GDP – while halving its carbon emissions. Explore why the language you speak can make you more or less likely to save for retirement, how one country is creating a nicotine-free generation, and where drone technology is used to grow new forests. Together, we will explore the places of peak happiness, health and abundance – and catch a glimpse into how they came to be the way they are.

Because whether you are suffering in a failed country or curious about how much better things could be, you deserve to live in Utopia.

To claim your copy, scan the code or visit www.amazon.com/dp/B0BT8HGVQV.

Made in the USA
Columbia, SC
24 November 2023

27076278R00090